"NOT" Seen On TV:

Real Estate Investors Guide

Creative Wealth Academy

www.RE90x.com 1-877-IGROWRICH

I look forward to staying connected in 2015!

TABLE OF CONTENTS

Chapter 1: Real Estate Guide 9
Real Estate Investing 11
Single-Family Homes vs. Other Property Types 13
The Fast Track 14
Long-Term Planning 16
Using Other People's Money (OPM) 17
Setting Your Goals 18
Getting Started 19
Real Estate Investor Tools 22

(Case studies with Harvard MBA Patty and Author Jerry) 26

Chapter 2: Finding Good Deals 27
Elements of a Good Deal 27
Sources for Locating Property 29
Property Characteristics 31
Classified Ads 32
Key Words to Look for in Classified Ads 33
Stay Away From These Words in Classifieds 34
Phone Techniques 34
Quick Survey Questions 36
Common Objections 37
Working With Realtors 37

Chapter 3: Evaluating Deals 40
Determining Fair Market Value 40
Quick Appraisal Techniques 42
Property Inspections 43
Post Property Inspection Negotiation 44
Property Inspection Script 45

Chapter 4: Real Estate Strategies 101 47
Basic Strategies 47
Contract Assignments 49
Sample Assignment Forms 50
Assignment of Contract 50
Assumable FHA and VA Mortgages 51
Wrap-Around Mortgages 54
Wrap Example 55
Lease Options 57
Option Agreements 58
Cash Deals 60
Cash Example 61
Foreclosures 62
Finding Foreclosures 63
The Foreclosure Process 64
The Foreclosure Clock 65
How the Property Is Held 66
How the Foreclosure Process Works 66
Foreclosure Terms 69
3 Types of Foreclosure Proceedings 69
Courthouse Research 70
Common Types of Liens 73
Priority of Liens 75
Foreclosure Notices and Documents 77
Profiting From the Foreclosure Process 78
Effect of Foreclosure on the Second When the Senior Forecloses 80
Effect of Foreclosure on the Senior When the Second Forecloses 81
Profit Before the Bank Foreclosure Sale 83
"Pre-foreclosure" 83

Sources of Buyers 84
The Perfect Target 87
Negotiating Like a Pro 88
Maximize Results 90

Chapter 5: Writing Contracts 92
Contract Considerations 93
Sales Contracts 93
How to Write a Purchase Contract 94
Sections of a Purchase Contract 96
Contracts for Purchase and Sale 101
Contract Presentation Checklists 103

Chapter 6: Mortgage Financing 106
Notes and Mortgages 106
Parties to the Mortgage 107
Mortgage Requirements 107
Mortgage Theory 108
Lien Theory 109
Title Theory 109
Trust Deeds 110
Mortgage Clauses 110
Types of Mortgages 115
Government Underwritten vs. Conventional Mortgages 116
FHA-Insured Mortgages 116
VA-Guaranteed Mortgages 117
Conventional Mortgages 118
Mortgages by Method of Payment 118
Standard Fixed-Payment Mortgage 118
Straight (or Straight-Term) Mortgage 119
Partially Amortized Mortgage 119

Mortgages by Payment or Yield Variability (AMLs, GPMs and SAMS) 119
Adjustable Mortgage Loan (AML) 119
Graduated Payment Mortgage 121
Shared Appreciation Mortgage 122
Mortgages by Purpose 122
Purchase Money Mortgage 122
Participation Mortgage 123
Blanket Mortgage 124
Reverse Annuity Mortgage 125
Package Mortgage 125
Home Equity Loan/Equity Line of Credit 126
Mortgages by Lien Priority 126
Mortgaged Property Transfers 127
Transfers Subject to Mortgage 127
Mortgage Assumptions 127
Mortgage Assignments 128
Default and Foreclosure 128
Default 128
Foreclosure/Public Sale 128
Foreclosure/Deficiency Judgment 129

Chapter 7: Investor Contacts & Groups 132

Appendix I: Sample Forms and Contracts 184

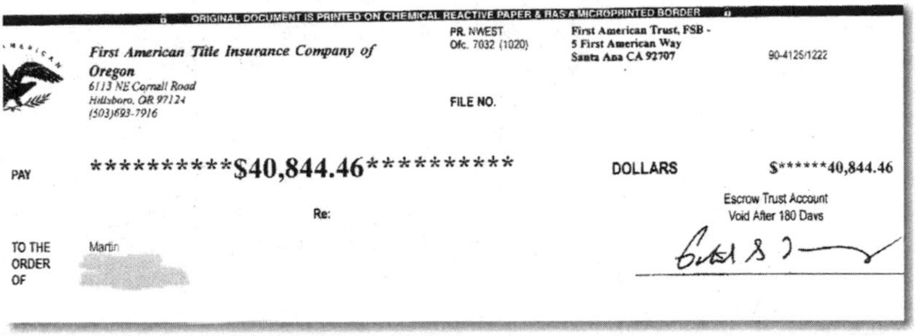

ORIGINAL DOCUMENT IS PRINTED ON CHEMICAL REACTIVE PAPER & HAS A MICROPRINTED BORDER

First American Title Insurance Company of Oregon
6113 NE Cornell Road
Hillsboro, OR 97124
(503)693-7916

PR NWEST
Ofc. 7032 (1020)

First American Trust, FSB -
5 First American Way
Santa Ana CA 92707

90-4125/1222

FILE NO.

PAY **********$40,844.46********** DOLLARS $******40,844.46

Re:

Escrow Trust Account
Void After 180 Days

TO THE ORDER OF Martin

The business works; you just have to work the business. Working the business means finding deals and making money. In one check, people make more than some do in one year. Throughout the book, you will see a few case studies with our team. Nothing flashy about the business, just real facts.

Meet the Authors

Brad Quintana was born and raised in Sandy, Utah starting out in the fitness industry where he quickly excelled to upper management making a six-figure income and overseeing a 64,000 square-foot facility with about 2,200 members per day. Brad, at age 19, began his investing career by providing Private money on multi-million dollar commercial deals, and working with high net worth individuals. He continued diversifying and learning from the top Real Estate Investors in the country, making his decision to leave the fitness industry to go full-time as a Real Estate Investor at 22 years old.

Brad currently resides in Draper, Utah with his wife of 11 years (Amy) and his three children (Rylan 7, Shaylee 4, and Kyler 1).

Chad McCall was born and raised in a small farming community, Morganton, North Carolina. After surviving a near fatal car accident, A country boy at heart, his life was changed at age 14, when a tragic accident nearly took his life. Defying odds and over-coming a disability, he went on to play collegiate and professional tennis.

Chad currently resides in Draper, Utah with his wife of 9 years (Ashley) and his two children (Blaze 9 and Cruze 2).

Brad and Chad decided to take control of their own lives at early ages. They both purchased real estate as teenagers (Brad 19, Chad 14), to later realize this would be the starting point of their journey together. As partners, they created their own destiny. Together since 2002, they have managed to facilitate more than 2,200 transactions all across the United States, and have clients residing in Canada, Mexico, Australia, South Africa and the

United Kingdom.

Brad and Chad have used partnering successfully to show people how to generate wealth. Partnering with an already strong, dedicated business, with like-minded owners, is your ticket to REAL SUCCESS!

CWA Mission Statement

The Creative Wealth Academy consists of an accomplished team of experienced professionals in key positions. The Company will continue to acquire and develop quality partnerships, properties, and funding on realistic values for its own investment affiliates, as well as its joint venture partners. These real estate activities will take place in selected targeted markets throughout the United States. The Company will provide all of the skills and systems necessary to maintain a full service real estate buying, selling, education, and management service to the highest standards of quality, to achieve the greatest operating efficiencies and, finally, to realize the highest profit performance. In all cases, CWA will maintain the highest level of personnel and support them with the most advanced systems. Talented and skilled professionals, who insist on only the highest standards, using the most sophisticated systems, and working in an intense but enjoyable environment, showing true application and not just theory, will lead and direct the Creative Wealth Academy.

Chapter 1: Real Estate Guide

Welcome!! You are about to move into the league of the best and most successful real estate investors. Real estate investing is truly one of the best businesses in the world! With more than 40 years of combined experience as business owners, real estate investors, educators, and entrepreneurs, we still have not found an equal to what this business can do compared with other business ventures and the capital it takes to get involved. Think about it, the only thing you have to invest in, outside of an education, is a phone, a computer, and a car, all things that you already have. Investing in real estate is not only the best way to build wealth, but it also provides you the ability to keep more of the money you make. Many entrepreneurs have picked real estate as their vehicle to make millions of dollars simply because there are so many different avenues, and so many possibilities, to achieve success.

The TV shows and their producers have created numerous shows that have different concepts like rehabbing homes, buying homes, selling homes, flipping homes, and many more. The most popular shows are those that introduce others to the world of investing into real estate. The problem is the true ups and downs with the business, aren't explained in their entirety.

This can lead many beginners into a very unforgiving business. Unanswered questions like:

- Where do you find the best deals?
- Where do you get the money to purchase investment properties?
- Do you use a legal entity to acquire the home?
- How many hours does it take to remodel a property?
- Are there permits and paperwork needed to remodel a home?
- The TV personalities and hosts, are they actors or actual investors?
- The laws and regulations in each state are different for investors aren't they?
- What are the tax implications with investment properties?
- What's the average time it takes from start to finish on these homes?
- Were there any resell restrictions or seasoning rules on the homes purchased and sold?

This guide is designed to provide you with a good understanding of real estate, to teach you creative financing and negotiation strategies, and to provide you with the knowledge and tools you need to successfully build wealth through real estate investing. The topics covered in this guide include:

- Real estate terms
- Locating property
- Evaluating deals
- Targeting good deals
- Negotiation techniques

- Contracts and offers
- Mortgages and financing options
- Creative financing strategies
- Risk-free contracts
- Purchase offers and specialty
- Discount mortgages
- Property management

By using these materials, you will gain knowledge about how to make money in real estate by using strategies for creative financing, limited money down, no money down, negotiation, and contract-closing skills. To get your feet wet, fill out example offer worksheets and contracts. Practice your negotiating skills by talking to sellers to become comfortable with this process.

If you are going to become a successful real estate investor, it's important to dedicate a certain amount of time each week. For instance, one or two evenings a week totaling around 5 to 10 hours weekly. Your investment in time and application will pay off in the long run. Make the commitment now to change your future forever.

Real Estate Investing

If purchased properly, real estate is one of the safest investments you can make. When the population continues to increase over time, people will always need a place to live. Perhaps you help out a first-time homebuyer or rent your property out; there is always money to be made in any real estate market.

In most parts of the country, real estate historically has increased by an average of 4 to 5 percentage points each year; that is, until the recent market crash. Understand, there will always be occasional downswings and decrease in property values, but historically, the market rate has continued to increase over time, for decades and decades. As long as people need a place to live, the trend will continue. Real estate is also affected by the rate of inflation. Inflation has leveled off in recent years, but the trend has been for inflation to increase, and it will do so again. For years, the inflation rate continued to drive prices up on real estate. In fact, those of us who own real estate right now look forward to increased inflation to drive up values on properties we currently hold.

Even in slightly depressed markets, great opportunities exist for making money in real estate. We call it "forced appreciation." When a property is priced at a high discount compared with the fair market value (FMV), there is only one way for the property value to go ... up. In many cases, it has less to do with what's happening in the market, and more to do with how knowledgeable you are and your ability to apply and use negotiating skills. When making a deal, knowledge, timing, negotiation skills, and money will always be the main factors in how much money you make when you sell.

Real estate always has been, and will continue to be, one of the best tax strategies for most Americans. Individuals can deduct the interest on their mortgage payments, thus reducing the amount of tax they owe.

One of the greatest advantages of investing in real estate is the power to leverage your money and investment. For example, you can tie up a $100,000 asset (property) with

$1,000 of your own money because you know a few real estate strategies. When the property appreciates in value, it appreciates on the $100,000, not the original investment of $1,000. Therefore, you "leverage" the property. The investment is even more valuable if the property is rented out. The monthly mortgage payment is paid by the renter, so someone else is paying for your equity growth in the property. This is the best use of "other people's money" (OPM).

Single-Family Homes vs. Other Property Types

The information in this guide is applicable to most types of real estate ventures. You can assign a contract for a commercial property, lease-option an apartment complex, or use the negotiation tactics for any real estate property. However, we suggest you begin your real estate investing in single-family residences (SFRs) because they have distinct advantages for novice investors, including:

- There are single-family homes for sale in almost every marketplace. Events happen in property owners' lives — such as job transfers, unemployment, divorce, or death — that indirectly create opportunities for the investor. These situations create big property discounts.
- The market is large. The demand for homes and shelter is growing in most markets. Therefore, you can usually turn a good deal around in a short period of time — especially if the sale is well-structured or at a discounted price.
- Limited management skills are required. If you invest in apartment complexes or multi-unit dwellings, property management problems increase. Investing in single-family homes reduces the need for management skills. In most

cases, the property will be sold, assigned immediately, or rented out using a lease-option contract to reduce tenant problems.

- Single-family homes are the easiest to borrow against. Home equity loans (HELOC) are common in the single-family property market. This can allow outstanding opportunities for financing and pulling equity out of a property. We prefer a HELOC over a refinance for amortized mortgages, but this will depend on your exit strategy.
- Many of you will not know much about multi-family dwellings, apartment complexes, or commercial real estate, but chances are, you know something about homes. Start with what you know. There will be opportunities for other investments later, when you have more experience and venture capital.

The Fast Track (NOT Seen On TV)

The fundamentals of real estate investing require:

- Understanding what makes a good deal and provides a sufficient return on investment (ROI).
- The ability to locate and negotiate profitable deals.
- The ability to appraise, analyze, and structure a good transaction.
- The ability to prepare and present a contract.
- Knowledge of what to do with the contract to turn a profit.

One of the most overlooked aspects in the process is "what to do with the contract." During the evaluation, review, and preparation, keep the ultimate objective in mind: "What is my exit strategy to make money on this deal?" The answer to this question will typically fall into one of three categories:

- **Short-Term Wholesale — Assign:** You just want to "quick turn" the property for immediate cash as soon as you put it under contract. This is a good place to start.
- **Mid-Term Rehab — Buy, Fix, Sell:** Major or cosmetic repairs that you simply got a great deal on that you want to turn around. Sell lower than high (FMV) to move inventory.
- **Long-Term Rental — Buy, Fix, Hold:** Creating a residual income along with appreciation and equity growth.

As you begin to evaluate properties, you'll come across the opportunity to do each of these types of deals. With every deal you look at, keep in mind the outcome as you structure the deal and/or offer.

Most likely, your initial goals will be to:

- **Acquire Immediate Cash:** Because of the time value of money, $10,000 cash in hand is more valuable than a $10,000 note to be paid out over time. If possible, try to pull some short-term cash out of each. Cash in your hand will motivate you and give you the means for diversification. Let the real-estate-generated money pay for your deals rather than hard-earned, day-to-day money that you have saved.

- **Solve Current Problems:** Perhaps you want to supplement your income or get out of debt.
- **Develop Buyers:** Begin to develop a database of buyers, understand what they want, and then go find it for them.
- **Reward Yourself:** To make it fun, set up a series of personal rewards when you buy, sell, assign, or acquire a property. Build your real estate trophy case!

Long-Term Planning

Once you complete a few "fast cash" transactions and establish a successful track record, begin planning your mid- and long-term investing strategies:

- **Build Mid-Term Income:** Through the short-term transactions, you will find buy-fix-sell properties that can now be purchased (you can purchase with cash if you want, thereby cutting out fees and producing a larger ROI) using short-term-generated money that will produce a larger profit per transaction.
- **Build Cash Reserves:** Make it a practice to put a percentage of your profit (10%-20%) from each transaction into an investment account for future real estate investing, marketing, etc.
- **Build Your Credit:** Work with existing credit cards to increase your credit limits. Start acquiring new lines of credit from additional sources.
- **Build Long-Term Income:** Through the short-term transactions, you will find good buy-fix-hold properties that

produce a positive cash flow in neighborhoods that will continue to appreciate in value.

- **Build a Team:** Develop a team of trusted professionals that has an understanding of what you are trying to do and can assist you in your investing activities (for example, title companies, Realtors, appraisers, home inspectors, property managers, real estate attorneys, insurance agents and accountants).
- **Build a Portfolio:** Create a portfolio of good properties that, in addition to producing income, creates a tax shelter and appreciates in value to provide a hedge against inflation.

Using Other People's Money (OPM)

As you begin your journey of investing in real estate, keep in mind that most successful real estate investors use other people's money (OPM) rather than their own cash. Hold out for no-money-down or limited-money-down deals rather than using a chunk of cash when you don't have a large cash reserve. Leverage, good financing and extended loan terms can help you achieve this goal:

- **Leverage:** Look for deals that allow you to control real estate using little to none of your own cash — especially when you are focused on short-term deals (such as transactional funding).
- **Maximum Loan-to-Value:** Try to get the maximum funding if possible on each property that you locate (100% financing).

- **Fixed Interest Rate:** The best loans have fixed interest rates and are assumable without qualifying.
- **Long-Term Loans:** Although short-term loans reduce interest fees, long-terms loans offer lower monthly payments that produce positive cash flow.

Setting Your Goals

There are many ways to make money in real estate, and as you obtain a better understanding of the industry, you'll uncover a variety of opportunities. Start by determining what your specific goals are. For example:

- Add an additional $5,000-$10,000 monthly to your income.
- Buy your own home at a large discount.
- Create a long-term residual stream of income.
- Buy an investment property to create a tax shelter.
- Become a full-time real estate investor.

Setting your goals now will help you stay on track. Take the time to list out your goals for the next 90 days to 12 months. Focus on this year first, then you can set your goals accordingly. Do not overwhelm yourself with inflated, unrealistic expectations.

My goal in the next 90 days:

My goal in the next 6 months:

My goal in the next 12 months:

Getting Started

Although this course will give you with the knowledge and tools you need to become a successful real estate investor, hands-on experience is always the best form of training. This list will help you get out there and get started:

1. Pick up real estate magazines at the grocery store to get a feel for prices in the area.

2. Drive for dollars! Look for "For Sale By Owner" (FSBO) signs and take down the phone numbers. Find other properties in the area and see what they are selling for.

3. Make copies of the Property Data Form and the FSBO Questionnaire to gather the important information you need to cover when making phone calls.

4. Acquire a local real estate purchase contract. Check with a local office supply store or the board of Realtors. Make sure you also get a copy of the addendum form.

5. Invest in some letterhead and business cards to let people know who you are and that you are a serious investor.

6. Find and review the classified ads in the newspaper and circle ads that have motivated seller phrases (need to sell, assumable, desperate, transferred, etc.). Find FSBO ads. Going through the classifieds on a regular basis will give you a feel for the marketplace and enable you to identify good deals.

7. Review the telephone scripts (see the "Phone Techniques" section) and practice them out loud or with a friend a few times. Start making phone calls to homeowners to see how much information you can get over the phone. Don't schedule an appointment yet, just try to get the forms filled out as best you can. Don't worry if you don't say everything right the first time or if you forget to ask something. Don't change your voice tone and make it sound like a sales call because sellers will pick up on it quick and you will lose deals. Just be yourself!

8. Once you have called 10 to 20 homeowners, make an appointment to review a property. Get a clipboard, notepad, flashlight and pen and go out to the property. Don't attempt to negotiate. Just get used to viewing property and filling in the property information form.

9. Evaluate the property. Can you assign the property? Structure limited money down to put the deal under contract. Once the forms are filled out, you will then be able to figure out the best possible option to make money on the deal. You have now bought yourself time to structure a deal the right way (even though you already have an idea of what strategy you want to use).

10. Draft a contract or agreement. Double-check the figures and clauses. Make sure you have a couple of escape clauses (i.e., subject to partners' approval). Submit the offer to the homeowner and see what happens. Do they ignore the offer or let the deadline expire? Do they counteroffer? If they don't respond to the contract, put them in a database with a note to check back in 30, 60 or 90 days. Things change over time, and the seller may become more motivated if better offers do not materialize.

11. Contact local Realtors. Use the Realtor script. Attempt to find Realtors who want to work with you or specialize in distressed property. Establish a good rapport.

12. Drop by a title company and/or a real estate lawyer. Check out their fees and services. Ask about volume discounts and the process in general.

13. Examine your credit profile and increase your available credit.

14. Take your banker to lunch. Let him or her know that you are beginning to invest in real estate. Ask for timely information about interest rate changes, areas to invest in the local market, bank properties, and potential investors. The rapport you build with your banker is as important as the information.

15. Call some rental properties advertised in the newspaper and speak to the landlord. Find out why they're renting the property out. If the answer is, "I couldn't sell the property," you have an excellent prospect. Ask the question, "Would you sell the property?"

16. Develop a database of buyers and spread the word among your contacts. You may even post flyers or ads to acquire a buyer's database.

17. Check out the "money available" section of the newspaper. A number of the individuals offering cash invest in real estate and may be a good source of cash, contacts and/or properties. The same is true of the "money for mortgages" section (for example, "We buy mortgages").

18. Drop by the courthouse. It is not as scary as you might think. Research your own property or a friend's to learn how the system works. The clerks will help you the first time or two, or at least point you in the right direction. Check out the Recorder's Office and inquire about which office handles tax and mortgage foreclosures.

19. Attend a foreclosure auction.

20. Review your materials at regular intervals. Keep your goals in mind. Most important, keep your commitment to spend a certain amount of time examining real estate, studying strategies and learning more about the industry.

Once you start applying these principles, you'll find out what you already know and what you still need to learn. Refer back to your guide as often as necessary, and don't be afraid to ask questions. If you make it a habit to look at properties, you will increase your ability to figure out what a good deal looks like, which will create more money-making opportunities. You will even find ways to make money on deals most investors will pass up. There is almost always a way to make money on a deal. We follow a list of 58 ways to locate properties on a weekly basis, and with this many avenues to find a good deal, there are many opportunities you just need to figure out what works for each deal. Someone will make the deal work, why not you?

Real Estate Investor Tools

No matter what business you are in, you will need proper tools if you are to be a success. The TV shows avoid the tools you will need to get started. Here is a list of essential tools:

1. **JOB OR BUSINESS OF YOUR OWN.** As you know, we talk about real estate making you wealthy in 5 to 10 years. In the meantime, you need money to support yourself and your family. A regular job or a business also makes it possible for you to obtain credit and appear credible to agents and vendors.

2. **KNOWLEDGE OF THE LAW.** Be sure to have in your possession a copy of the relevant legislation for your state. Read the documents thoroughly. Although you will be using a lawyer, there will be times when you will need an answer and the lawyer will not be available. It is also good business to have some knowledge of the law, which affects your business.

3. **FILING CABINET.** It is very important to be organized. You must be able to lay your hands on any documents in a hurry. The best way to do this is to use a filing cabinet for all your papers. The filing cabinet should be legal size to accommodate typical real estate forms. In the filing cabinet, you should have legal forms, records of properties you have visited, rental studies, people who can assist you, articles concerning real estate, receipts for expenses, rental records, and so on.

4. **AMORTIZATION TABLE.** This is very small and you will probably carry it with you. In this book, you can find the information you will need to calculate mortgage payments once you know the interest rate and the length of the amortization of the mortgage.

5. **CALCULATOR.** A calculator will come in handy when doing quick calculations to determine cash flow and prices for properties. A financial calculator would be preferable because it would eliminate the need to use an amortization table.

6. **OFFERS TO PURCHASE (agreements of purchase and sale).** You can buy these forms at any legal stationary store, and some real estate brokers will even give them to you. By having these forms available at all times, you will be able to take advantage of opportunities that may come along while you are out for a walk or when your agent is on vacation. Since the forms are standard, the seller and his lawyer will readily accept them. You should change them to suit the particular purchase, but the basic form is always the same.

7. **AGREEMENTS OF PURCHASE AND SALE FOR CONDOMINIUMS.** There are special terms that only apply to condominium purchases, and you should have these forms in the event that you buy a condominium or townhouse:

8. **STANDARD LEASE FORM.** One form is provided in this guide. Also, these are available at any legal stationary store or from your lawyer.

9. **SMALL CLAIMS COURT FORMS.** You can obtain these free from any small claims court office. If it should become necessary for you to sue a tenant, you would need to fill in the form, call the court office and learn how much money would be needed to process the claim. Next, take the form and a certified check to the office. Later, you will go to court and prove your claim.

10. **BOOKS.** You should have as many books as possible on real estate, tenants, property management, home inspection, and so on. For questions, call 1-877-IGROWRICH. *"The book you don't read, can't help you."*

11. **HOME OFFICE.** This provides positive tax deductions.

12. **COMPUTER.** A computer can create professional documents, house a buyer's database and provide marketing materials. If you have real estate evaluation software, you can analyze cash flow, project profit and track properties.

The Fast Track Flow Chart

What is a good deal?

How to locate a good deal:

- **Realtors**
- **Real Estate Magazines**
- **Newspaper**

Appraise, inspect, and analyze

Prepare contract

Present contract:

- **Owner**
- **Realtor**

What do I do with my contract?

Close and buy property

Assign Contract

Fix up and sell

$$ PROFIT $$

Patty ▸ **The Creative Wealth Academy**
Just a note to say that Ray is the best! After seeing my posts he gave me a call to make certain I had seen Chad's training video on how to build a killer cash buyers list. Now that is support! Thanks, Ray!

Like · Comment · Share · 10 hours ago ·

, Brad Quintana, Ray Colledge and 2 others like this.

(Case studies with Harvard MBA Patty and Author Jerry)

Jerry
Thanks Chad McCall & Brad Quintana that was a great trip. I appreciate the time you spent with me this week, not to mention the Jazz game. Next time let's do that in Phx where it's 70 degrees and we have a few casinos and golf courses around ☺
It was great to spend time with these guys. They don't operate on hype and pipe dreams. It's simple. There's a ton of whole selling going on, now lets try to capture 1%.

Unlike · Comment · Share · Unfollow Post · December 6 at 6:38pm

Chapter 2: Finding Good Deals

Elements of a Good Deal

What Is A Good Deal?

Real estate is similar to any other type of investment. There is an essential investment amount (down payment or purchase price of the home), a return on investment (cash flow from rent, tax savings, and/or appreciation), and risk (market risk or trend analysis) involved. Your objective is to maximize your return on investment while minimizing the risk. There are some general guidelines for determining good real estate deals.

10-10-10 Rule

A good rule of thumb is the 10-10-10 rule. Never put more than 10% down on a property. Tie up as many properties as you can with the lowest investment possible. Never finance or assume a loan with an interest rate over 10%. The interest can kill you in the long term. Always require a minimum of a 10% discount off of the fair market value, not the listing price. Fair market value (FMV) is the price that comparable homes are actually selling for in the community today.

Positive Cash Flow

If you invest in rental properties, be sure the cash flow per year returns at least 20% after mortgage, interest, tax payment and other homeowner expense (e.g., maintenance, repairs, utilities and homeowner association dues). Otherwise, you should consider a straight investment in another financial vehicle.

The 60% Rule

Look for property you can acquire at 50%-60% of FMV. If you get a better discount, that's great. But at least you'll know that, if you buy it at 50%-60% of FMV, you'll most likely be able to turn it around fast at around 90%. Understanding your market is very important, because the % below FMV may be 65%-70% in a competitive market. Quick turnaround time on your investments is important, especially in the beginning when you may be cash-strapped and can't afford to hold onto the property for long.

Other Elements of a Good Deal

- A first mortgage and any other mortgages that are assumable/no qualifying (FHA or VA) or private mortgages (old or new seller take-back): If mortgage is not assumable, anticipate a greater discount.
- A property in good condition and ready to rent (i.e., move-in condition): If the property is not in good condition, deduct three months' rent and the fix-up costs from the purchase price.
- Property in long resell markets: Discount the price 10% for every four months of resell.

- Property that produces a positive cash flow: The rent must cover PITI (principal, interest, taxes, and insurance) and maintenance. The remaining cash should be a 20% yield on cash down, otherwise the price must be lowered.

Example:

Down payment: $10,000. Price you pay: $100,000. Net cash flow must be $2,000 per year. (Mortgage seller takes back $90,000, payment $9,000 per year ... Total rent: $18,000, less real estate tax ($2,000), less other expenses ($5,000). Net cash flow: $2,000 per year. Property value: $150,000 (which makes the conversion ratio 6%). The margin of profit is 33.33%, aka a good deal!

Sources for Locating Property

There are many of sources for locating property (with our proven systems we have over 58 ways to locate a good deal). We will cover a few of them here, to get you started. You need to understand that on TV you see a home that has been possibly in consideration for several months prior to being seen on TV. Realistic expectations must be set, when locating a goo deal.

The best place to begin your search is the local newspaper, and the best properties to focus on are For Sale By Owner properties. Begin your search with this group of sellers. Specifically, search the classifieds for ads that provide insight into the owner's motivation. Focus on motivated sellers who may already have moved, been transferred, or just need cash quickly.

The second place to search is the "Homes for Rent" section in the newspaper. In some cases, these properties are being rented because the owner could not sell the property and needs the monthly cash to pay the mortgage. If you ask the question, "Would you like to sell the property?" you may hear some "Yes" answers.

The third place to look is in specific neighborhoods. Simply drive through target neighborhoods and look for "For Sale By Owner" signs. You will find many.

You can also call on properties listed by Realtors, but keep in mind that Realtors will typically complicate the negotiations and require a healthy commission for their efforts. Following is a partial list of property sources:

- Real estate magazines: Typically available free of charge in supermarkets, restaurants, convenience stores and other public places.
- Newspapers: Sunday is usually the best day for real estate classified ads.
- Realtors: Small mom and pop companies are the best selection. They are typically more flexible.
- Phone book: Look for Lender-REO (real estate owned) departments, banks and savings and loans, builders, property management companies, investment companies, and estate or trust attorneys.
- Courthouse, town hall, and registry of deeds: Look for *Lis Pendens* (foreclosure) files and/or legal advertiser publications that list foreclosure notices.
- HUD, VA, FHA, FNMA, and FHMC local offices
- IRS auctions and sales

Property Characteristics

Before you hit the market, you should have a reasonable idea of what to look for initially.

Keeping in mind that you want to sell the property within a reasonable amount of time, look for the average home. Stay away from the high end of the market. The selling process can be unreasonably lengthy. Moreover, the low end is also to be avoided unless you have the expertise and time to spend on a fixer-upper. The middle range provides the best opportunity to turn the property around quickly.

Characteristics:

- **3 bedroom/2 bath (3/2):** Ideally, the property will be a mid-price range 3/2, which is the typical home for the average family of two adults and two children.
- **Middle price range:** Novice real estate investors can get easily distracted from the ideal property to buy and resell. The low price of a fixer-upper or the potential windfall of a high-priced property may tempt you. You can make money in the low and high ends of the marketplace; however, the easiest, safest sweet spot for novice investors is the mid-range market. Mid-range properties are in higher demand and tend to sell faster. The challenge with the low end of the market is the time it can take to resell the property. If it's a fixer-upper, the time required to repair the property (two to four months) may cost more than you anticipate. Then you have to market and sell the location, perhaps another three to six months. At the high end of the market, the sales cycle is longer, perhaps six to 12 months of marketing.

- **All the right things wrong:** Unless you're an experienced builder or construction worker, the property should be free of damage and require only cosmetic repairs (paint, wall paper, carpet, landscaping, cleaning, etc.). However, if the deal is really good, more extensive repair work can be considered.
- **No major repairs required:** Unless you're really handy, stay away from properties that require major repairs (roofs, plumbing, gutting, etc.).
- **"We care" neighborhoods:** A run-down house in need of cosmetic repairs in a "we care" neighborhood is a jewel for an investor. Look for properties in communities and locations where families would like to live. The community may include a church, park, schools, and a community watch and association. These types of communities are easy to spot. Look for kids playing in the park and in yards, clean streets and well-tended lawns and gardens.

Classified Ads

A great place to start is the local newspaper or in real estate publications. Hundreds of properties are sold through the classified ads. They are readily available and, with a few insights, you can focus on the most important ones. Classified ads can be in print form or online. Both methods are necessary.

Sample Classified Ads

Orange City – Owner Transferred! 4 yr. Old home. 3br 2 bath. Split W/pool. Family room. Workshop, Sprinkler. Must Sell Immediately Call Owner at 555-555-1212	Deland – Reduced by $13,000. Owner desperate. All serious offers will be considered. Creative financing considered. Call owner at 555-555-1212
Apopka- Open house Sunday 1-4 p.m. 145 N. Olympic. New kitchen. Sun Deck. New carpets. Near park and schools. 3/2 split. Owner financing. Call 555-555-1212	Altamonte Springs – 2200 sq. ft. 4/2. Beautiful home on golf course. Many extras. VA assumable. Non qualifying. Call 555-555-1212
Deltona – Motivated owner says just make an offer. 4/2 split. Lg. Master bedroom. New roof. Moving need to sell quickly. Call 555-555-1212	LONGWOOD – By Owner. New carpet 3br/2ba. Screen porch. Nice park. Willing to consider a lease option to the right person. Call 555-555-1212
Winter Garden- Builder close out. My loss is your gain. I'm very motivated to sell my 2 last homes. Consider owner financing. 4/2 W/pool. Brand new. Call 555-555-1212	Oveido – Must sell! Spotless home. Great for families. Great location. 4/2. Large Screen porch. Lots of backyard. Low down payment. Lease option OK. Let's talk. Call 555-555-1212

Key Words to Look for in Classified Ads

Price reduced	For Sale By Owner (FSOB)
Non-qualifying Loan	Nothing Down
Must Sell	Out of Town Owner
Desperate	Out of Town
Moving	Motivated Seller

Transferred	Will Sacrifice
Illness Forces Sale	Repossession
Bankruptcy	Estate Sale
Foreclosure	Investment Property
Below Market	Distressed Property
Below Appraisal	Seller Anxious
Vacant	Reduced
Divorce	Handy Man Special
Needs Work	Make Offer

Stay Away From These Words in Classifieds

Gorgeous	Immaculate
Oversized Den	Newly Renovated
Ceiling Fans	Mint Condition
Wall-to-wall carpet	Appraised Value
Walk-in Closets	Custom Work
Gorgeous Fireplace	Great View
Large Bedrooms	

Phone Techniques

If you were to call on every property available in your market and visit every home, you would go crazy. It would take forever, and you would never find the gems in real estate. A telephone script, a quick survey, and a record form are your best tools to maximize returns on time and effort. Following are sample script and quick survey forms to help you weed through available properties quickly and locate the best opportunities.

Script #1 General:

"Hi, my name is _______. I am a real estate investor and would like to discuss your property for sale. Is now a good time? (If not, schedule a conversation.)

I'm looking at several properties and just need to take a few minutes to see if your property would be of interest to me." If your survey determines that it is a good deal, put an offer on it within 24 hours.

Script #2 FSBO — Already Moved:

"I am a cash investor. I try to solve the problems that many sellers face. Maybe I can be of help to you, too?

The inactivity of real estate agents causes longer selling times for a house ...selling time that could drag on for months and even years. As time goes on, it costs you a lot of money to keep paying the mortgage payment on a house you no longer want, and with real estate commissions, you end up getting less for your property than you should. Even if you take a chance with a Realtor and find a buyer, the buyer would have to qualify for a new loan. If they don't qualify, you wasted your time and paid additional mortgage payments for nothing. If a buyer does qualify for a mortgage eventually, you still end up waiting and paying a 7% real estate commission. You also pay interest payments for the time you have to wait while the Realtor is trying to find a buyer and you pay 3% in closing costs such as lawyer fees and other costs. Your total expenses add up to 20%, or even more. What we do is pay you cash and hope we can make a good profit, although there is always the risk we may lose money. Do you think we might be able to get together?"

Quick Survey Questions

- In what area is your house located?
- Why are you selling?
- How long has the house been for sale?
- Are you in a hurry to sell (any deadlines)?
- Are you flexible on terms?
- How much do you think your house is worth? How did you come up with the price?
- How flexible is your price if we brought you a cash offer?
- What is the balance of your mortgage? (Equity should be a minimum of 30%.)
- What type of mortgage? Interest rate? Assumable FHA or VA?
- Would you consider carrying back financing (owner take-back [OTB] or second mortgage)?
- How quickly do you want to close?
- What are you going to do with the money? (Leave this question for last because sellers typically think this is nobody's business.)

Common Objections

- If the homeowner does not want to provide the information you request, say: "I don't want to waste your time or mine, and I'd like to put an offer on the property as soon as possible. This is a common discussion in the sale of a property." (Ask next question.)
- If homeowner wants you to see the property, say: "I would love to after I get the answers to a few more questions."

Your time is valuable, so don't waste it!

Working With Realtors

In most cases, we suggest that you work directly with the owner. The best reasons to do your own negotiations are (1) to ensure you are represented correctly and (2) to reduce the cost of the transaction. Realtors require a commission that could inflate the cost of the property. However a Realtor can be an asset if they understand what you're looking for and are prepared to work with you in the acquisition of the property. Finding a good, flexible Realtor can take time. It may take a few attempts before you find one you can count on — one who understands your plan and is prepared to work with you. Making one or two Realtors part of your team can be key to your success.

Following are a few questions that can assist in developing the Realtor relationship:

1. We buy a property at 30% to 40% below fair market value for cash and quick closing. Do you handle property from distressed sellers who need to sell quickly and can be

bought below market value? (If the answer is no, don't waste any more of your valuable time.)

2. Do you know of any properties that can be bought below market value now?
3. Who do you know who has property of this type for sale?
4. How about properties with fully assumable FHA or VA mortgages? Can you find some?
5. We want to assume no-qualify mortgages. However, an all-cash deal is OK. We will close quickly at the right price.
6. Are you familiar with HUD and VA bidding? Do you get these lists weekly, and are you registered to bid?
7. Are you familiar with county and city down-payment assistance programs for first-time homebuyers?
8. Are you familiar with local FHA guidelines and "Sweat Equity Programs"?
9. Will you work with us if we re-list the property with you?
10. Can you recommend a good appraiser, surveyor, termite company, lender, title company, etc.?
11. Can you call me back with some good deals in a few hours?
12. Let's make some money!

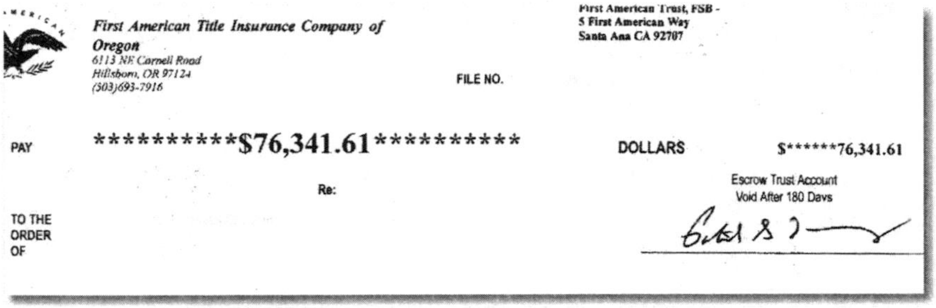

First American Title Insurance Company of Oregon
6113 NE Cornell Road
Hillsboro, OR 97124
(503)693-7916

First American Trust, FSB -
5 First American Way
Santa Ana CA 92707

FILE NO.

PAY **********$76,341.61********** DOLLARS $******76,341.61

Re:

Escrow Trust Account
Void After 180 Days

TO THE
ORDER
OF

(Case study with Martin)

Chapter 3: Evaluating Deals

Determining Fair Market Value

The key to investing in real estate and structuring a good deal is your ability to know the fair market value (FMV). Keep in mind that the asking or listed price is not necessarily the fair market value, but simply what the seller wants. On the cable channels you don't see the negotiation with the sellers or if the Realtor has a pocket listing. The price could have been pulled from the air, or the Realtor may have suggested it, but buying right is very important. You have to know the ways to determine the value if you don't have a good realtor on your team. Following are four quick ways to determine the FMV:

1. **Comparable Sales:** Contact a Realtor and ask for some comparable sales in a specific community or area. Realtors have access to past sales records and can provide you with a list of the most recent sales on comparable properties in an area. This will give you an idea of the FMV in the community. There are many resources online for comparable prices, be careful since things can vary drastically.

2. **Courthouse Records:** A visit to the courthouse can help you find the recent sale information for houses in a specific

community. In some areas, you may also be able to access this information online. Research properties with the most recent sales in a community.

3. **Tax Assessed Value:** The county government tracks property values to assess property taxes each year. However, most tax assessments are below market value. If you do an average in your community, you'll find they are consistently at a rate below market value (for example, 80% of market value).

4. **Professional Appraisals:** Professional appraisers, for a fee, can provide an appraisal or estimate of what a property would sell for under normal market conditions.

   The most basic and commonly used method of value estimation of a single-family residence or a duplex/quad is the comparable method.

For single-family homes:

- Use a minimum of three comparable homes that have sold in the area within the last three to six months (They don't have to be all in the same subdivision as the property in question, but at least one or two of them should be). Make sure to use actual sales information from a Realtor or courthouse records rather than what the seller or their neighbors tell you houses have sold for.

- Use tax-assessed value, and factor it by 80% to 85%.

  Example:

  If property is assessed at $65,000, the tax assessor usually values it at 80% to 85% of the actual FMV value. To determine the market value, divide the assessed value by the "percentage."

Assessed Value / Assessment Percentage = Market Value

$65,000 / .80 = $81,250 Market Value

The amount of the assessment is shown directly on the tax bill.

Quick Appraisal Techniques

In addition to the standard evaluation techniques of comparables, courthouse records, tax assessments, and appraisals, the fair market value of a property can be evaluated in a number of other ways. Most techniques evaluate the return on investment or are used to "code" an ideal property. There are a number of quick and easy coding systems that can help you evaluate properties:

- **Quick Appraisal:** The quick appraisal system codes the mid-range property according to a simple A-B-C system. The A property is the middle range property in your community — the ideal property for resale and marketing.
- **Profit Margin:** The profit margin of a property is the fair market value minus the purchase price and is quoted as a percentage. A 40% to 50% profit margin is a fair deal with room for error. Even if the property needs work, there is still room for profit.
- **Conversion Ratio:** The conversion ratio is a simple system of looking at the cash invested into the property and the equity in the property. Anytime you can find an investment that returns three times the equity of the property, generally the property is a good choice.

Typically, there are set real estate investment guidelines to consider when estimating profit expectations.

Property Inspections

Any property you purchase should be inspected by a professional. Make sure all your contracts have a "subject to inspection report" clause. For properties you actually plan to purchase, don't cut corners by using your local handyman or Uncle Fix-It. Hire a professional because you never know what's under the roof or carpet. The TV shows in most cases have inspected these homes several months in advance before acquiring the property for use, it just doesn't happen by chance they can assess the home in 20 minutes, especially if it needed a $50,000 remodel.

However, you may decide to use some informal inspection techniques to get a feel for the property and perhaps initiate the negotiation process. To complete this exercise, you will need some general knowledge, a clipboard, paper, pen, flashlight, ball bearing, and an inquisitive attitude.

Following are a few inspection tactics that can help you lower the price, by kicking the tires a little. As you walk through the property, take detailed notes and investigate the entire property:

- **Roof:** Prior to entering the home, stop outside and examine the roof. Look for signs the roof may be damaged (e.g., dry rot or shingles curling up at the edges). Three or more years of life remaining on the roof is recommended.
- **Ceiling:** Once inside the property, examine the ceiling with your flashlight. Look for water damage, stains, or fresh

paint on the ceiling. If you find a blemish, highlight the area. Don't say anything. Look at the spot very intensely, and sooner or later, the homeowner will say something like "Oh, we fixed that."

- **Cupboards:** Check the cupboards. Look under the sink. You might even pause under the sink or look twice.
- **Ball bearing:** Inspectors will use a ball bearing to test the levelness of the property. Put a ball bearing on a counter or flat floor surface to determine if the property is level.
- **Inspection report:** Once the inspection has been professionally completed, use the report to renegotiate the purchase price.

  As a general rule, look in every corner and cupboard on the property. Document all the blemishes and problems. You will use them to justify your discount. You might even supply an estimate of costs attached to the purchase offer.

Post Property Inspection Negotiation

Make sure all your contracts have an inspection clause. For example, "Subject to inspection and written acceptance of the inspection." Always specify a time frame for the inspection (e.g., "within 10 days from acceptance").

Most people don't know what to look for when evaluating a property for problems and concerns. A good cleaning and a paint job can hide a lot of damage. Under the roof could be termite damage, water leakage, and infestations. Plumbing can be old and outdated. The electrical system may be a fire hazard. How do you know? Get professional help — a professional inspection.

Upon receipt of the inspection report, estimate the cost of the repairs for the damaged areas, and evaluate if this will affect your decision to purchase the property. If the damage or concern is expensive to repair, you may want to pass on the property. It can be difficult to turn around a badly damaged property. On the other hand, if the damage is small, you can use the report to renegotiate a lower price for the property. Simply review the problems with the owner and ask that the owner pay to repair the property. Since the repair will take time and effort, the property owner will most likely opt to drop the price.

Buying a property as-is is the most lucrative way to purchase the property at the best price. Conveying the discount to the seller is the only challenging part. The conversation can't put the seller on the defensive, but must have your best interests in mind.

Property Inspection Script

"Hi, this is_______. I have received the inspection report back from the professional inspector. I am still very interested in purchasing the property; however, he raised some major concerns. Apparently:

1. The roof needs to be repaired at an estimated cost of $2,000.
2. The garage door is broken and will cost about $800 to fix."

At this point you have a couple of options available ... and both work:

- **Option #1:** *"Do you want to repair the damage before we close on the property or would you prefer to reduce the cost of the property to offset the damage?"*
- **Option #2:** *"What do you think we should do from here?" (Wait for a response.) "Perhaps you could reduce the price of the property by the repair cost. This way, we can stay on schedule for closing, and I can deal with the hassle of repairs instead of you. Fair enough?"*

(Mike and Lisa $49,000, in one month)

Chapter 4: Real Estate Strategies 101

Basic Strategies

There are hundreds of real estate strategies and offers. The structure of the real estate deal is the function of the property, the owner's motivation, financing, the type of loan, the market, and your own creativity. These are rarely, if at all mentioned, on a TV show.

Traditionally, there are several templates of good properties to consider and negotiate for.

First, remember that you are looking for the ideal property (for example, 3/2, "we care" neighborhood, 10-10-10, no major repairs, mid-range price). After you have qualified the property by these characteristics, focus on the following:

- **Contract Assignment:** A contract assignment is a good way to get started with no money. Negotiate a good deal and simply assign your rights to another buyer for a fee.

- **Assumable VA or FHA Mortgages:** These properties are a good selection due to the ease of financing and lack of credit qualifications if the property qualifies. Check the date of the original loan to see if the property is a good choice. These are not a very common type of property.
- **Wrap-Around Mortgages:** In this case, you use the owner's financing and qualifications to keep the mortgage on a property. The owner could establish a new mortgage on the property. Take in the monthly payment and then pay the original mortgage. This may not be legal in some states.
- **Lease Option:** No money for a down payment? A lease option is a great way to acquire the property with as little down as possible.
- **Options Contract:** Establish an option on the contract. You can sell the contract or hold on to the contract and exercise the right later.
- **Foreclosures:** The market is large. Often, the selling prices are 40% to 50% below fair market value. Occasionally, a 50% or greater discount can happen. An understanding of the process can help you profit.
- **Cash Discount**: Great deals are much easier to find if you have the cash to acquire a property quickly.

If you focus on these beginning strategies, you can make your investment in real estate very profitable. Once you have successfully completed several of these types of purchases, you can attempt more creative and unique negotiations.

Contract Assignments

An excellent strategy when funds are tight is the assignment of a contract. A contract assignment is a simple and powerful moneymaker that simply requires a little contract knowledge and good negotiation skills.

Characteristics:

- **Step 1:** Negotiate at 80% (20% discount) or less.
- **Step 2:** Set a long closing date (90-120 days minimum).
- **Step 3:** Use the phrase "and/or assigns" after your name on the purchase offer/contract.
- **Step 4:** Include a clause that ensures you an "out option" or "escape clause" (i.e., subject to partner's approval).
- **Step 5:** Find a buyer for the property.
- **Step 6:** Assign your rights to purchase the property for cash and charge an assignment fee.
- **Step 7:** Inform the seller of the change (use Assignment Form).

By using the words "and/or assigns" behind your name, you have the right to transfer your rights to purchase the property for cash.

This is an interesting technique to generate cash and profit. You don't need any cash to buy the property. The person you "assign" the contract to buys the property. You sell the contract for cash. A contract assignment can be executed at any time before the contract expires.

Sample Assignment Forms

Find below a sample letter to the original owner and an assignment contract:

Dear ____________,
This letter will confirm our conversation earlier today by phone indicating the assignment of my contract with you for________________________________ to ____________________________ at the following address: __________________________________. You will find a check enclosed from Mr. / Mrs. ____________________ for $________ to redeem the promissory note in this contract. All the terms and conditions as originally agreed to in the contract remain in full force and effect, including the settlement date, scheduled for ________________. If you have any questions, please contact me at __________ (W) or __________ (H).
Sincerely,

____

Assignment of Contract

By this assignment of contract, and in consideration of an earnest money deposit of $______________, ________________(original buyer) hereby exercises his/her unqualified right to assign all of their rights, obligations, and responsibilities in the above noted, dated ______________, with_______________ (owner) to a new buyer, as follows:

The new buyer of this property hereby agrees to fulfill all of the same conditions and terms of the above referenced contract, including but not limited to all settlement requirements as originally stated and noted above.

The total consideration for this assignment is $___________, to be paid at settlement.

Original Buyer ________________Date____________

New Buyer ____________________Date____________

Notary:______________________________

The new buyer of this property hereby agrees to fulfill all of the same conditions and terms of the above referenced contract, including but not limited to all settlement requirements as originally stated and noted above.

The total consideration for this assignment is $_______________, to be paid at settlement.

Original Buyer ___________________

New Buyer ______________________

Date ____________________________

(Get this document notarized.)

Assumable FHA and VA Mortgages

If credit is an obstacle or if you just want to reduce the turnaround time for financing a property, assumable VA (Veterans Affairs) or FHA properties may be the ideal investment. Nowadays, they are rare, so when you find one, get excited! There are all kinds of opportunities surrounding these types of homes. To fully understand the benefit of finding these gems, you must understand a little about their financing and obligations:

- **VA Loans:** The government has made lending a little easier for our nation's veterans. VA loans are guaranteed by the government in case of default and usually have a limited- or no-money-down payment (i.e., on the original note/property). To qualify, the veteran must live in the property originally, but can move out later. VA loans made prior to March 1, 1988, have the additional distinction of being easy to transfer. Transfer of a VA loan involves assuming the mortgage (non-qualifying for loans prior to March 1, 1988) and paying a $45 assumption fee. Loans originated after March 1, 1988, require the new homeowner to qualify for financing. For individuals who can search out, find, and negotiate a good deal, assumable VA properties can be a gold mine.
- **FHA Loans:** The Federal Housing Association is an agency of the government that helps new homeowners acquire property. The government essentially insures that, if the homeowner-occupant defaults, the government will make good on the loan. There are limitations on the amount of funds insured, and the process is time-consuming. But there are some interesting benefits, including the potential of a very low down payment. Prior to December 15, 1989, FHA property and loans were fully assumable and non-qualifying. Again, there is an outstanding opportunity for acquiring the property with minimal qualifying and easy financing options. Loans originated after this date require the new owner to qualify for financing.

Assuming you can find these types of properties (VA or FHA mortgages that are non-qualifying and assumable), the outstanding opportunity is to acquire them with no financial qualifications. Therefore, the only obstacles are your ability to structure a good deal and to finalize a quality negotiation.

Let's look at an example of how to structure a property purchase.

VA Example

Characteristics:

- Asking price: $128,000
- VA assumable and non-qualifying
- First mortgage has $102,000 left; 30 years original; 10% interest; 21 years, 9 months left.
- The homeowners want $26,000 cash because they want to retire and move to a beach apartment.

OPTION #1

You can pay the $26,000 and simply assume the first loan for $45. The homeowner will send away to the mortgage company for the assumption package. You would start making payments on the first mortgage. The only major negotiation is who pays the closing cost ($1,200 to $2,000). You could split the costs, have the owner pay, or you can pay. This option is quick and easy. Simply send the information to the title company with a copy of the purchase offer and/or agreement, and you have a new home.

OPTION #2

The first mortgage is assumable and non-qualifying. The $26,000 is negotiable. One option may be to ask the homeowner to take back a second mortgage for $26,000 or whatever you can negotiate. The interest rate is negotiable. The term (number of years or months) is negotiable. For example, perhaps you pay $500 to $1,000 as a down payment and finance the balance for 10 years at 8% interest. It is really up to you and the homeowner to agree.

OPTION #3

Cut the best deal you can for the down payment, interest rate, and length of the mortgage. You might even have the homeowner throw in extras: refrigerator, stove, washer, dryer, drapes, furniture, TV, or whatever you want. Ensure you have the words after your name "and/or assigns." This will give you the right to sell the rights to the purchase of the home to anyone for money (the same as an assignment of contract). Perhaps you'll assign the contract without the TV — a bonus for your den.

Wrap-Around Mortgages

Let's assume a situation to understand this strategy and how it may help you buy or sell a property. The seller has a home that has a fair market value of $100,000, with $60,000 in an assumable mortgage (qualifying), 8% interest, and $40,000 in equity. You may try to discount the property by 20% and get the owner to take back a second mortgage for the balance of the equity. This would keep your out-of-pocket cash to a minimum — a good objective. It may even be very attractive if the first mortgage is assumable and non-qualifying. But what happens if you cannot qualify? Perhaps you have bad credit, not enough credit history, or too many properties already leveraged to qualify.

A solution could be the wrap-around mortgage. In this case, the owner of the property could establish a wrap-around mortgage on the property at your recommendation. The wrap-around mortgage, sometimes called an all-inclusive trust deed (AITO), is a mortgage on the property at whatever terms you agree to. Perhaps you can negotiate an $80,000 mortgage at 8% for the next 30 years. The homeowner gets paid the monthly mortgage payment on the wrap-mortgage of $587.01. In turn, the owner pays the first mortgage of $440.26. The homeowner has a regular income of $146.75 and is really receiving 8% on their investment. Not too bad considering what the owner would get on a bank certificate of deposit (CD). Because the seller actually finances the deal, there is no qualifying. However, the seller may ask the buyer for references, accounts, and checks.

Now, as a smart seller, you would want to do your homework check references, bank accounts, possibly qualify the buyer, and get guarantees. As the seller, you might consider this option if you have a qualified buyer and if you can get some favorable terms. For example, because there is no qualifying for bank financing, you might ask for a sizable down payment, or you might increase the interest rate above the norm, thus getting a better return on your money. After all, the worst that might happen is that you would have to foreclose on the property and get it back.

Wrap Example

Characteristics:

- FMV: $100,000

- First mortgage qualifying: $60,000
- Individual has lost a job and wants to move back home.
- Credit still good, but the owner is worried of what could happen in the near future.

Note: *To implement this strategy, consult a real estate lawyer in your state. You may have to write a contract for deed, and you must review the existing mortgage on the property for any infringement of rights. For example, the initial mortgage may not allow a wrap mortgage and could be in jeopardy (if they find out about the wrap mortgage).*

OPTION #1

A key to the wrap mortgage, is understanding, what the owner will do with the money or what is motivating them to sell the property. Perhaps they need the money, perhaps they don't. If they have a fair amount of equity and are prepared to hold the wrap mortgage, you have an outstanding opportunity to pick up a property with limited qualifying. Certainly go for the 20% discount from the beginning of the negotiation. Ask the owner to hold the wrap mortgage at a fair interest rate. If they are concerned about the mortgage payment and potential credit problems, this may be a good alternative. Essentially, the owner is lending you the money to buy the house.

OPTION #2

It may be time to be more aggressive. Consider developing a wrap-around mortgage that will look after the first mortgage payment (e.g., $440.26 a month, $60,000 at 8%) and insert a balloon payment of $20,000 in five years at an acceptable interest — perhaps 10% simple interest. Remember, you have already discounted the property by $20,000. If the owner needs cash, you may consider a small down payment or even trade them some services (e.g., moving company or job counseling).

Lease Options

First-time homebuyers usually have a challenge buying property because they have no down payment. This is a problem that is easily taken care of by the lease-option strategy. Basically, the monthly rent or a portion of the rent goes toward a down payment at some point in the future.

Example:

- $1,000 monthly payment
- $900 to owner, $100 toward down payment (please be advised the Dodd-Frank Act must be taken into consideration)
- Price set now

  Three years from now, a $3,600 down payment has been created. The buyer will need to come up with the $96,400 or else pass on the option.

  Two separate transactions actually occur in this situation. However, the transactions can be included on one form.

1. **Lease Contract:** A standard lease or rental agreement is created for the property. It typically includes: length of lease, monthly rent, deposits and rights of the parties.

2. **Options Contract:** Allows you to purchase the property any time during the contract length. Usually the price is fixed at today's FMV, but it can be at any price (negotiation).

   The contract includes:

   a. Length of term (i.e., months, years, or a specific date of execution)

   b. Purchase price at the termination period

   c. Finance terms, if you are acquiring the financing from the seller

   d. Credit to be allocated to the down payment

3. **Notes:**

   a. Sample agreements are included in the contract section for review.

   b. Include "and/or assigns" after your name on the contract, so you can assign the contract.

   c. Make sure you record the option at the courthouse on the property; therefore, the property cannot be sold by the owner.

Option Agreements

An option contract on a piece of real estate basically provides the right to purchase a piece of real estate at a specific price with specific terms. Options must be in writing to preserve the legal rights of the buyer or rights of the owner. The contract is usually unilateral (the buyer can option the contract, but is not obligated to do so). The owner is obligated to sell the property under the contract for the period specified.

A lease option is a purchase to happen in the future meanwhile the property is leased by you (rented). There are several ways to take advantage of options. For example:

1. Locate potential commercial sites if you are a good judge of future development. Perhaps you can assign a variety of commercial land development sites. Simply put an option on the land with the owner for a few hundred or thousand dollars. Then locate a developer or commercial application.

2. Tie up the rights to land or property with an option. For example, when cellular phones were initially introduced, people looked for tall buildings to set up the "cell sites" antennas. A few wise people optioned the roofs of buildings and then sold the rights to the cellular phone companies. The options were for a few hundred dollars, and the resale was for thousands.

3. If someone has a prime property but does not want to sell, offer an option. You can option some cash now for a future right. Perhaps the person needs cash now for a future right you will exercise.

4. If you believe that, in the near future, the price of a property will increase dramatically, you may be able to inflate the purchase price of a property. Knowing that the price will increase in one or two years, you can tie up a purchase price that will be high now but low in consideration later. For example: The fair market value of a property is $100,000. You know the price will increase dramatically. So you suggest a purchase price of $110,000 in the next three years for an annual renewable option of $1,000. In two-and-a-half years, you exercise your option

of $110,000 when the FMV of the property is $120,000. You get immediate equity, or you can sell your rights for money.

A sample option contract is located in Appendix I. The contract is one-sided in your favor, not the seller's. You do not have to buy, but the seller has to sell. An option can have different legalities involved in each state, and when considering to enter into a lease option or exit a property through a lease option, please seek legal advice from a licensed professional in the area.

Please consider any and all regulations at the local, state, and federal level when considering lease options and any other type of creative seller financing strategy. The *Dodd-Frank Act*, released January 2014, is something you must be aware of in any case of selling or purchasing property, in a seller financed situation, including but not limited to a lease option.

Note: We are not trying to alarm you, but intend to raise awareness with the Dodd-Frank Act. A key point in this regulation is, if you are selling on a lease option, you can cause a conflict with this law, if the buyer is receiving any type of credit, discount, or payment toward the purchase of the property. If this is a part of your business or you are considering this please look into the Dodd-Frank Act further.

Cash Deals

Cash is King. If you have access to a lot of cash or if you have a partner who has cash available, this can be a profitable strategy. There are properties in the marketplace that may need to be turned around in a short period of time, maybe a few days or a week. They offer an excellent opportunity for profit. Expect a steep discount. Start the negotiations at 50%, and don't take less than a 25% discount off the FMV. An important caveat to this strategy is knowing that another property will be just around the corner. Do not panic: Do not fall into the "this is a once-in-a-lifetime opportunity" trap. There will be others. .

Once you have purchased the property at a substantial discount, turn it around quickly. This strategy works best if you have a pre-approved database of buyers looking for properties. A good plan once the property is acquired is to leverage the property and borrow the maximum possible on the property. You may even be able to borrow more on the property than you paid for it in the first place. It may require repairs, a new appraisal, or a new tenant.

Cash Example

Characteristics:

- FMV: $200,000
- Needs to have as much cash as possible due to potential IRS seizure.
- Closing date is in seven days.

Negotiate a deal at the lowest price possible. At least 25% discount. Don't risk your own money on this type of deal unless you have a lot of it. Perhaps a Partner can help you in the cash department. Do your homework: FMV, ownership research, outstanding debts, liens against the property, and post options.

Once you have the rights to the property, go for the quick sale. Keep your cash liquid. It is better to have 10 to 15 properties working for you than one big score because it minimizes your overall risk vs. reward.

Another option is to hold onto the property and attempt to take the cash back out in the form of a mortgage. Go to the bank and acquire regular financing. Normally, a bank only funds 70% of an investment property, but if it's priced and appraised properly, you may get all of the money back — perhaps more than you expected.

Foreclosures

Foreclosures are a fact of life. Any time a debtor breaches an obligation of a security document (e.g., mortgage, deed, or trust), the lender will take the steps to foreclose on the property. The grantor most likely does not want to acquire the property, but it does want to get repaid the funds owed. There is an orderly process to the foreclosure and, if possible, an opportunity to cure the situation. However, some homeowners are not in a position to cure the situation. This may happen because of a:

- Loss of job by one or more of the homeowners.
- Financial crisis — perhaps there is a need for immediate cash due to a health or family problem.
- Business failure or downturn.
- Divorce between couples, causing the need for property liquidation.
- Death of the property owner, which may force the property into foreclosure.

- Adjustable rate mortgages can increase quickly in times of high interest and result in the property owner failing to make the payments.
- Balloon payment (large payment) that causes a challenge for homeowners.
- Job transfer — the property may suffer because of the "two mortgage payment syndrome."
- Temporary negative cash situation.
- Out-of-state/out-of-town owner.

A fundamental key to making profit in the foreclosure market is to understand why the property went into foreclosure. Perhaps the owner just has a temporary cash shortage. You may be able to help them and take an equity position in the property in return for rectifying the situation. Or the owner may be financially devastated and just wants to dump the property before their personal credit is destroyed. You could help them solve their immediate problem and give them a new start.

Finding Foreclosures

There are many sources to aid you in finding foreclosures. Hopefully, you can find the foreclosure before it has gone too far into the foreclosure process. Find below a few locations to begin the search:

- Classified sections
- Legal newspapers
- Attorneys

- For Sale By Owner — FSBO
- Realtors
- Auction companies
- Banks — REO departments
- U.S. Marshals Service
- Listing services
- IRS auctions
- Bankruptcies
- Probate court
- Your own advertising
- County courthouse, town hall, or registry of deeds:
    a. Check for "new cases"
    b. Check for "sale" file

The Foreclosure Process

In the United States, there are approximately 12 ways to foreclose on a real estate property. Each state has its own procedure and method of execution. They fall into the following major groups:

- Mortgage Lien and Judicial
- Mortgage Lien and Power of Sale
- Trust Deed Lien and Power of Sale
- Trust Mortgage Title and Power of Sale

- Mortgage Intermediate and Judicial
- Trust Deed Intermediate and Power of Sale
- Mortgage Intermediate and Power of Sale
- Mortgage Intermediate Strict Foreclosure
- Trust Deed Lien Judicial
- Mortgage Title Judicial
- Security Deed and Power of Sale
- Mortgage Title Entry and Possession

Each state has a specific system — a step-by-step process for the lender and the owner to follow in the foreclosure process. It is a good idea to understand the specifics of your state's process and the minor nuances.

The Foreclosure Clock

A. Foreclosure starts

B. Lis Pendens

C. Complaint

D. Default

E. Final judgment

F. Sale date

G. Right of redemption period

How the Property Is Held

Generally, real estate is secured by either a debt or a lien, often called title theory or lien theory. Title theory states classify the mortgages or trust deeds for properties as contracts, and contract law applies. The contract conveys the title to the property secured by the underlying debt. In lien theory states, the mortgage or trust deed is a lien against the property. A lien just means an entity (usually a bank) has a claim or hold on a property as security for a debt. Liens are an encumbrance to the property and recorded against the property. You may have more than just one lien (debt) against a particular property.

How the Foreclosure Process Works

The lender follows a specific system of foreclosure to repossess the property or rectify the satisfaction of the debt. The states are split approximately 50/50 on the process.

First, there is Power of Sale. A good portion of the trust deed states use Power of Sale. Power of Sale tends to be a less expensive and quicker way to foreclose on a property. Under Power of Sale, the lender (trustee) informs the property owner that the debt has not been paid and specifies a due date. In a few weeks, if the payment has not been processed, a stronger demand for the payment is issued, often an immediate demand for payment. States regulate the period of time prior to public auction, approximately four weeks.

The process is sometimes complicated by FHA and VA properties. FHA and VA properties are guaranteed by the federal government through their respective programs, and have their own regulations and procedures for rectifying the debt obligation and listing of the properties. A deeper understanding of the FHA and VA process is encouraged. There are some outstanding opportunities in the FHA and VA foreclosure markets.

Contact your local branch office for more information.

Judicial foreclosure governed by the courts accounts for the other half of our nation's foreclosures. Note that Power of Sale states usually have some form of judicial procedure.

Although slightly different in approach, both systems have essentially seven steps:

1. **Non-Payment.** From time to time, we all may be a little late in our mortgage payments. The penalty for being two weeks late may be a $10 or $20 late fee and perhaps a mention on our credit report. Beyond two weeks, the lender starts to get a little anxious. They may let a month slide, with notice of non-payment, but very quickly they begin to take the non-payment seriously. The second month, they will send notification of past due, and approximately six to eight weeks after the non-payment, you can expect the phone to start ringing. The lender will try to solve the problem and work out a plan for repayment.

2. **Default.** If payments continue to go unpaid, the note is moved to a default setting. Legal action is initiated: A demand letter asks for full and immediate restitution of the debt owed or else the attorneys will file suit to foreclose.

3. **Lis Pendens.** After default, a Lis Pendens (legal notice) is filed against the property. The Lis Pendens will include the following: case number (assigned by the court), lender (plaintiff), owner(s) (defendants), property, legal

description, notice of foreclosure, and the attorney for the plaintiff.

4. **Complaint.** The complaint lists the events that took place to force foreclosure, including mortgage amounts owed, time frame of non-payment, listing of the parties and property, a complete history of the mortgage, and reference to the official documents. At this point, the note is accelerated. The entire amount of the mortgage and related costs is due.

5. **Judgment.** Final judgment occurs after a set period of time determined by the laws of the state. The defendant can still rectify the situation by paying the default. All fees have to be paid, including non-payment court fees and legal costs. This does not mean negotiations can't happen (by the owner or an investor). The lender will file a motion for judgment. When final judgment is granted, the plaintiff has the right to sell the property.

6. **Sale.** After judgment, the motion of sale is put into action. An order for the sale is processed and a specific date for public auction is set.

7. **Redemption Period.** The process of foreclosure can take anywhere from three months to a year from start to sale. Note that, during this time, the legal fees and costs are escalating and being attached to the property. However, an investor can acquire the property at any point during this period. Obviously, sooner would be favorable to later (due to less legal expenses and mounting costs). It changes by state, but generally, investors can intervene up to the day of the sale. On the day of the sale, a bidding war can erupt.

Foreclosure Terms

Foreclosure is a legal proceeding instituted by a lien-holder to enforce the lien against the debtor when he or she is in default of the debt or charge or fails to perform some act to which he or she is bound. Foreclosure results in a public sale of the property covered by the lien, with the proceeds of the sale used to pay (satisfy) the lien-holder's claim. Foreclosure also terminates all rights of the debtor in the property, including the debtor's right of equity of redemption. (True in most states.)

Equity of redemption is the right of the debtor during the foreclosure proceeding and before the public sale to redeem his or her interest in the property after it has defaulted by paying the full debt plus interests and costs.

Some states have statutory redemption, which gives the foreclosed debt or equity of redemption a certain period of time after a public foreclosure sale. The foreclosed debtor must pay the full sales price plus interest and costs to redeem interest in the property.

3 Types of Foreclosure Proceedings

- **Judicial Foreclosure:** A judicial foreclosure is the process of enforcing a lien by filing a foreclosure suit in court.
- **Non-judicial Foreclosure:** A non-judicial foreclosure is the process used in some states of enforcing a lien through a Power of Sale, which is a clause in the lien giving the lien-holder the right to conduct the foreclosure and sell the property without filing a foreclosure suit in court. Under this type of foreclosure, the lien-holder

advertises the property and holds a public sale to sell the property.

- **Strict Foreclosure:** A strict foreclosure is the process used in some states of enforcing a lien. Under this process, the lien-holder gives the delinquent debtor notice of default and files the appropriate documents in court. The court then establishes the amount due on the lien and orders the debtor to pay the defaulted debt in full within a certain time. If full payment is not made within this time, the debtor's equity of redemption is foreclosed (terminated) without a sale of the property, and title to the property is awarded to the lien-holder by the court.

Courthouse Research

In *title theory* states, the sale of the property, auction, or foreclosure takes place at the courthouse. The foreclosure process is threatening to the homeowner, and occasionally, concerns may rise for the lender, but these should not scare you at all. It is a systematic and well-defined process. At regular times of the day and week, the court auctions off the property (the sale). To find the auction times, simply call the office and ask the clerk. You have probably heard the statement that the property was "sold at the courthouse steps." In fact, it probably was sold in the lobby, foyer, or a specified location. A typical procedure (sale) would involve:

- A scheduled time for properties to be sold
- A clerk making an announcement of file case numbers and their statuses (solved, available, etc.)

- A clerk listing the case and/or property description and asking for bids, which is followed by bidding; the property is bought and paid for at the courthouse.

Note that the property will usually have at least one bidder. The lender wants to ensure the property is sold for at least what is owed on the property. Therefore, the lender or their designate starts the bidding at the amount being foreclosed. If that is the only bid, the auction is over. The lender will actually receive the money, so there is no real cost. There have been occasional errors where the lender did not protect its debt and a bidder other than the lender received the property for a song. If there are multiple bidders, the process can be quite entertaining.

We recommend that you visit the courthouse and watch several auctions. You will learn a lot about the process. You may even try to get to know some of the other individuals at the auctions. Banks, lawyers, agents, investors, title company representatives, and more will often be in attendance, and they are all excellent contacts for an investor. If you own a property, check the property documents while you are at the courthouse. Just ask the clerks. It will help if you have the legal description, and you can get it from the mortgage documents. Also, review the bulletin boards in the offices, and pick up any publications and notices in the offices. Check the Lis Pendens list (legal notice of foreclosures).

In title theory states, the lending institution holds title to the property in the name of the borrower through a Deed of Trust. A Deed of Trust is a legal document that embodies an agreement between a lender and a borrower to transfer legal title to real property to an impartial third party, a trustee, to security the payment of the borrower's debt. The trustees controlling the title of the property can control the location of the sale, which may or may not be at the courthouse. Usually, the trustees publish notices of sale locations.

There is a lot of opportunity for profit in foreclosure. Certainly, you can buy a property during the foreclosure process, prior to sale at a discount. As the foreclosure clock is counting down to the sale time, there are opportunities for great deals and negotiations. Here are a couple of examples:

- Joint venture with the owner. The owner may have had a temporary setback. The owner could have a substantial amount of equity in the property. Perhaps you can approach the owner to help solve their current problem, get their payments back on track, and save their personal credit profile. In return, you might agree to take a 50% ownership of the property. Alternatively, you could agree to sell the property and get cash out for both you and the owner. In this case, you would want to get to the owner early in the foreclosure process.

- Look for properties with substantial equity. Usually the lender will set the opening bid just over the loan value to ensure the debt is paid. However, the property may have a lot of equity. If so, you can pick the property up for a major discount and resell the home.

- Approach successful auction winners and ask if they would be willing to sell the property — perhaps on a lease option or an installment sale.

In a *lien theory state*, the deed stays with the borrower (the mortgagor), and the lender (mortgagee) places a lien on the property based on the type of mortgage. A lien is a form of security interest granted over an item of property to secure the payment of a debt or performance of some other obligation. It is a legal right that a creditor or a unit of government (city, county, state or federal) has first position over specific real and personal property of a debtor as security for repayment of a debt or charge, or for performance of some act to which the debtor is bound.

A property owner may voluntarily create a lien, such as pledging the property on a mortgage lien in order to secure a loan. Liens may also be involuntarily created, such as a judgment lien arising out of a legal proceeding against the debtor to enforce a debt that has been defaulted or a tax lien against the property by the government. A lien does not transfer title of the property to the lien-holder.

Common Types of Liens

- Real estate tax liens are filed against real property for non-payment of property tax.
- Special assessment liens (municipal improvement liens) are filed against real property for improvements such as street paving, sidewalks, and sewers. A lien for an improvement not completed is a pending special assessment lien; a lien for a completed improvement is a certified special assessment lien. Generally, special assessment liens are levied only against those properties that will benefit from the improvement, and in an amount apportioned according to the cost of the benefits received, rather than by the assessed tax value of the property.
- Federal estate tax liens and state inheritance tax liens accrue against real and personal property at the time of the death of the owner.

  Note: Real estate tax, special assessment, and federal estate tax liens are imposed by law without consent of the owner. They are superior liens because, once they are filed with the Clerk of the Circuit Court, they take precedence over all other types of liens.

- Federal income tax liens may be filed against real and personal property for non-payment of federal income taxes.
- State corporate income tax liens may be filed against corporate real and personal property for non-payment of state corporate income taxes.
- State intangibility tax liens may be filed against real and personal property for non-payment of the state intangibility tax on such items as stocks, bonds, and mortgages.

  Note: Federal income tax liens, state corporation income tax liens, and state intangibility tax liens are by law without consent of the owner, but take precedence only from the date of filing with the Clerk of the Circuit Court.

- A judgment lien is a lien rendered by a court in lieu of monetary compensation awarded to a plaintiff against a defendant as a result of a suit.
- A mortgage lien is a lien placed on real property voluntarily by a mortgagor (owner of real estate) as security for repayment of debt.
- A vendor's lien is a right of a vendor (seller of real estate) to repossess the property sold until the buyer makes all payments for the full purchase price. A vendor's lien right is waived if any other form of security for the debt has been received.

  Note: Judgment, mortgage and vendor's liens take precedence only from the date of filing with the Clerk of the Circuit Court.

- A mechanic's lien is a lien for labor, materials, supplies, or repairs to construct or improve a property.

Note: Mechanic's liens filed with the Clerk of the Circuit Court date back and take precedence over mortgages given after the date the first supplies or materials were delivered to or repairs or labor were performed on the property, mortgages given during the progress of construction, or mortgages given within 90 days after the last supplies or materials were delivered to or repairs or labor were performed on the property. .

Priority of Liens

In a foreclosure, certain liens may be superior (senior) and certain liens may be inferior (junior) to the lien being foreclosed due to provisions of laws or date recording of the liens. The example below illustrates the priority of liens in a foreclosure.

Example:

A vacant residential lot was purchased for $20,000 cash on January 15. On February 20, the owner entered into a contract with a builder for $80,000 to construct a home on the lot. Construction on the home started on March 1. On April 12, the owner obtained a construction loan from a savings and loan association in the amount of $75,000, which was secured by a mortgage lien on the property. On May 5, a special assessment lien of $1,000 for sidewalks was certified by the city. Construction was completed on August 10, and $16,000 was due the builder because of changes and addition of an enclosed swimming pool requested by the owner. On September 1, a judgment lien was filed against the property for $12,000 based on a delinquent credit card account debt of the owner. On September 8, the special assignment lien was foreclosed because of non-payment. None of the liens has been paid. The proceeds of the sale are $90,000 and are distributed according to lien priority, which is:

1. Special Assessment Lien (May 5) $1,000
2. Mechanic's Lien (dates back) $16,000
3. Mortgage Lien (April 12) $75,000
4. Judgment Lien (September 1) $12,000

The proceeds of $90,000 are sufficient to pay off the special assessment lien of $1,000 and the mechanic's lien of $16,000, as well as to pay $73,000 toward the mortgage lien of $75,000. No money will be paid toward the judgment lien. The mortgage lien-holder (the lender, or Beneficiary) and the judgment lien-holder (the credit card company) must now look to other real and personal assets of the owner (the trustor) for their claims.

Once the mortgage is paid in full, the trustee conveys the title to the trustor, who then owns the property free and clear.

If the trustor fails to make the payments, the Beneficiary notifies the trustee that the payments have not been made, and the trustee puts the property into default. The Beneficiary is the person who decides the timing for the Notice of Default. It could be one (1) day, but usually closer to 60 or 90 days. Once the 90 days have passed, the Beneficiary notifies the trustee that the note is in default, and the trustee files the Notice of Default with the county recorder's office.

This triggers a three-calendar-month period — not 120 days, but three exact calendar months. Then comes Stage 2, which is the publication period. This is where the possibility of the property being auctioned becomes serious. The trustee must publish for three consecutive weeks, or 21 days, in a paper of general circulation. At the end of the 21 days, an approximate sale date is set and an auction is held, and the property will be sold to the highest bidder.

All cash is required at the sale. There is no catching up on payments. The lender is entitled to all cash. The auction can be held at the courthouse or another public place that is convenient to buyers. The location of the sale is published in the Notice of Sale in the newspaper. Bidders must show a cashier's check in the amount of the final judgment or default amount, or larger, depending on the bid.

Foreclosure Notices and Documents

Notice of Default: The foreclosure process begins when a lien-holder files a Notice of Default. The Notice of Default names as defendants the debtor and anyone else who may have rights or interests in the property covered by the lien. The Notice of Default identifies the debt and the lien securing it and states that the property is in default.

Notice of Lis Pendens: Concurrent with the filing of the Notice of Default, a Lis Pendens is filed on the public records in the county where the property is located for the purpose of giving notice to all persons that the title to the effected property is in litigation and may become subject to foreclosure.

Public Sale: The public sale is usually a sale at auction upon notice to the public of the sale. The sale is usually conducted at the county courthouse.

Proceeds From Public Sale: If the proceeds from the public sale exceed the lien-holder's claim and any junior liens, the debtor receives the excess money, sans any unpaid property tax liens and expenses of the sale. However, if the proceeds are less than the lien-holder's claim, a deficiency exists. In this case, the lien-holder may request the court to enter a deficiency judgment against the debtor for the balance due. A deficiency judgment gives the lien-holder (creditor) the right to attach the judgment as lien on the debtor's real and personal property and, if necessary, foreclose on the judgment lien to obtain the balance owed. (Deficiency judgments are not available in some states.)

Deed in Lieu of Foreclosure: To avoid the trouble and expense of foreclosure proceedings, a debtor who is in default on a lien may voluntarily deed the property covered by the lien to the lien-holder (creditor) if the lien-holder agrees to accept the title. The debtor should receive a letter from the lien-holder that cancels the unpaid debt. A deed in lieu of foreclosure does not extinguish the rights of any lien-holder whose lien is senior or junior to the lien in default.

Profiting From the Foreclosure Process

There are basically three ways that you, as a real estate investor, can effectively work with property that is in foreclosure or property that has been foreclosed upon and has been retained by the lender:

1. Bid successfully on a piece of property at the foreclosure sale.

2. Negotiate a contract on a property with the owner prior to the pending foreclosure sale.

3. Negotiate a contract with the lender, who has retained the property after the foreclosure sale. (Note: Often, this property has been turned over to a real estate brokerage firm to sell.)

   Each of the three approaches outlined above can lead to successful discounts on a property. Is one area better than the other to concentrate your efforts? That will depend on several key factors:

- Are you going to assign your contract rights?
- Are you going to "joint venture" the property?
- Are you going to hold "title" to the property?
- How much cash do you have available? (This could be your money or OPM, such as funding available for RE90x Deal Partners. For information about how to partner, go to www.RE90x.com/partner.)
- If you hold "title" to the property, what is your intent:
- Resale (short-term holding)?
- Hold for rental (short term, 2 to 5 years — resell)?
- Hold for rental (long term, 5 to 15 years — long-term market appreciation)?

Each area of foreclosure has excellent profit potential. The area(s) you choose to work in will be determined by what best suits your individual investment needs.

Effect of Foreclosure on the Second When the Senior Forecloses

Joe owns a property worth $100,000

Joe owes the bank a 1st mortgage: $60,000

$500/mo. P&I

Joe owes Bob a 2nd mortgage: $10,000

$100/mo. P&I

The Bank (1st mortgage holder) is foreclosing.

The property goes to a public sale.

The highest bidder will own the property. The proceeds of the sale will be paid to the first mortgage holder (bank) first; to the second mortgage holder (Bob) second; to the other lien-holders (if any) third; and the remaining proceeds will go to Joe (owner).

Mary, an investor, bids $65,000

Answer the following:

1) How much will the bank receive?$60,000
2) How much will Bob receive?$5,000
3) How much will Joe receive?$0
4) What happens to the 2nd mortgage?Eliminated

5) What happens to the 1st mortgage?Paid in full

Effect of Foreclosure on the Senior When the Second Forecloses

Joe owns a property worth $100,000

Joe owes the bank a 1st mortgage: $60,000

$500/mo. P&I

Joe owes Bob a 2nd mortgage: $10,000

$100/mo. P&I

Bob (2nd mortgage holder) is foreclosing.

The property goes to a public sale.

The highest bidder will own the property. The proceeds of the sale will be used to satisfy the second mortgage holder (Bob) first; other lien-holders (if any) second; and the remaining proceeds will go to Joe (owner). The high bidder now must make the first mortgage payment.

Mary, an investor, bids $15,000

Answer the following:

1) How much will the bank receive? ____________________
2) How much will Bob receive? ____________________
3) How much will Joe receive? ____________________

4) What happens to the 2nd mortgage? ____________________

5) What happens to the 1st mortgage? ____________________

Lien-holder has a lien against Joe

Joe owns three properties

Lien is against all three

(1) **(2)** **(3)**

You are interested in buying Property 1. You pay the lien-holder $500 to release Property 1. Lien still exists against two other properties (2 and 3). Lien-holder is now $500 richer.

1. Buy the property "subject to" lien.
2. Validity (some liens are not valid. Ask a real estate attorney or title company for advice).
3. Statute of limitations (laws vary from state to state).
4. IRS liens.

Profit Before the Bank Foreclosure Sale

"Pre-foreclosure"

Joe Owns a Property Worth $100,000

Bank Holds a 1st Mortgage $60,000

$500/mo. P&I – 10 months behind

Bob Holds a 2nd Mortgage$10,000

The Bank Is Foreclosing.

Sequence of Events

1. Contact Bob (the second mortgage holder).
2. Negotiate to purchase the $10,000 second mortgage from Bob for a discounted price ($1,000).
3. An "assignment of mortgage" will be prepared by a title company or an attorney.
4. YOU are now the second mortgage holder; your options:

1. Negotiate with and buy the property from Joe:
   A. Reinstate the first mortgage ($5,000 plus lender's expenses).
   B. Satisfy your second mortgage ("Satisfaction of Mortgage").
   C. YOU now own the property.
2. Reinstate the first mortgage and foreclose on your second mortgage.

A. **Possibility #1:** Joe (the owner) reinstates the second mortgage (pays $5,000 plus your foreclosure expenses). You now hold a $10,000 second mortgage for which you paid $1,000. You can hold for the monthly income or discount and sell the second mortgage for cash.

B. **Possibility #2:** Joe (the owner) gives you a "Deed in Lieu of Foreclosure." You now own the property.

C. **Possibility #3:** The property goes to a public sale.

If no one else bids, you will own the property. If anyone else bids, you receive cash.

Sources of Buyers

The strategies listed in this guide are much more effective if you have a ready-made market to sell the property. From the minute you begin negotiating property, making offers, and acquiring property, you must begin marketing property to the public. The sooner you have a collection of individuals asking you to find them properties, the better. Consider these four starting points:

1. Review the List of Potential Buyers

Begin by asking yourself, "Do I know anyone who may be interested in buying or investing in real estate?":

- Cash Buyer Data (provided to RE90x Deal Partners only; for information about how to partner, go to www.RE90x.com/partner)
- Fellow real estate investors (most have a list of applicants)
- CPAs, accountants, and business associates

- Property management firms (may have access to investors or buyers)
- Realtors or brokers
- Attorneys
- Doctors
- Engineers
- Other professionals
- Stockbrokers
- Investment counselors
- Corporate executives
- Successful business people
- Nothing down investors
- Fix-up investors
- First-time homebuyers
- Your boss
- Your friends
- Your relatives
- Section 8 Landlords

2. Secondary Sources

Consider the variety of real estate publications, and look for individuals who are actively investing. They may know of buyers or invest themselves.

3. Generating New Sources

- Civil and social activities
- Banking contacts

4. Advertising

- Go to www.RE90x.com and sign up to speak with a local investor
- Newspaper advertising
- Bulletin boards
- Penny Saver / Thrifty Nickel publications (free)

5. Bird Dogs (Deal Facilitators)

A bird dog is anyone who can help you find investors or buyers. You may create a reward system for people who bring you qualified clients, such as a free dinner, $50 cash, or a percentage of the deal. To find bird dogs, there are several ads you can place, examples of which are provided in the RE90x program. The following are samples of a few ads provided in the program:

- Make easy cash ad
- Courthouse researcher ad
- Put up signs ad
- Part-time job, full-time income ad
- Expired Non MLS listed Homes from a realtor

The Perfect Target

One of the best targets for purchasing your great real estate deal is the first-time homebuyer. Most first-time homebuyers lack money and have limited funds for a down payment and closing costs. Also, they are not familiar with the real estate process and need help.

As you build your database of individuals interested in purchasing property, take the time to gather their personal information and prequalify them with a lender. Generally, the purchaser will need:

- Down payment: Required minimum 3% of purchase price
- Income and job stability:
- Must have two years employment in same industry
- PITI payment = 28% of gross income
- Credit — willingness to pay:
- Must not be late on any payments
- No bankruptcy
- No foreclosure
- Total debts — inclusive of mortgage payments, secured debt, and unsecured debt — not more than 30% of gross income
- Satisfactory rent history
- Additional cash (for closing costs, prorations and utility deposits)

Negotiating Like a Pro

Some people believe that "how" you buy a property determines your profit. We agree. Your negotiating skills can determine your profit. In a wholesale deal, for example, you should have a buyer in line for the property, and that buyer has a specific price he or she is willing to pay you. When you acquire a property below that buyer's set price, you can count the difference as profit. Negotiation can be the deciding factor between a small profit and a large one.

You must develop negotiation skills to be a successful real estate investor. Use body language, strategies and tactics to maximize effectiveness. The following list may help you in your negotiations:

Appointment:

- Phone (be casual and listen more than you speak)
- In person (casual dress, collared shirt always for men)

Meeting:

- Be on time
- Dress appropriately
- Have all documents ready (two contracts filled out with different buying options)
- Greet politely
- Ask to look around the property
- Be friendly

- Seating arrangement (side by side)
- Have all parties present

Time to talk business:

- Inquire about the circumstances
- Listen and analyze the need
- Do not get involved with the problem
- Find a way to solve the need
- Present the proposal
- Be creative in objections
- Explain the benefits (understand people and what motivates them)
- Overcome objections
- Keep control of the subject
- Reinforce the problem (timelines, deadlines, negative alternatives)
- Narrow down alternatives
- Limited solutions
- Ask for decision
- Wait
- Compromise — find equal ground
- Reaffirm credibility — you are a professional investor
- Review the agreement in detail

- Do the paperwork
- Check everything on paper (twice)
- Sign documents
- Be honest and sincere in helping
- Use common sense
- Time is on your side
- Walk away. Don't get stuck! There are lots of other deals.

Maximize Results

Generally, individuals have one of two perspectives: short-term profits or long-term investments. The short-term perspective is a great way to increase your lifestyle, get rid of cash problems, and make you feel good. However, the long-term perspective is more satisfying. There is nothing better than waking up and not having to go to work! (That is, unless you really want to.)

Keep the short-term and long-term perspectives and suggestions in mind.

AT&T LTE
9:53 AM
Messages (2)
Mike
Edit
Can u fill me in on these? Michael
How are things? Just got in from Africa!
It's gonna be huge!
7:24 AM
(1/2) We closed on two of the properties and still waiting on the third. Hopefully by the end of this week when the contract expires. Can't wait to here about y
(2/2) our trip to Africa. Michael
You da man!
Text Message
Send

(Case Study with Mike and Lisa)

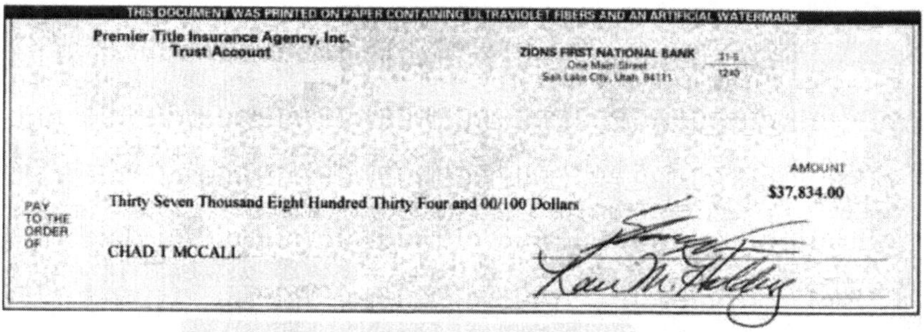

THIS DOCUMENT WAS PRINTED ON PAPER CONTAINING ULTRAVIOLET FIBERS AND AN ARTIFICIAL WATERMARK

Premier Title Insurance Agency, Inc.
Trust Account

ZIONS FIRST NATIONAL BANK
One Main Street
Salt Lake City, Utah 84111

AMOUNT
$37,834.00

PAY TO THE ORDER OF

Thirty Seven Thousand Eight Hundred Thirty Four and 00/100 Dollars

CHAD T MCCALL

($37,834 check, one of Brad and Chad's deals)

Chapter 5: Writing Contracts

Contract Considerations

Sales Contracts

- **Definition:** A written agreement between the buyer and seller for the sale and purchase of real estate.
- **General Rule:** If the buyer wants to buy and the seller wants to sell, they will close the sale. If either party wants to cancel the sale, he or she will find a way out.

Elements of a Sales Contract:

- Date
- Buyer's name
- Seller's name
- Deposit
- Purchase note
- Mortgages and liens taken "subject to"
- Terms and conditions

- Legal descriptions
- Signatures

Buying protection clause example: This contract is subject to approval by the buyer's accountant.

Selling protection clause example: This contract is subject to final approval by the seller's attorney.

How to Write a Purchase Contract (NOT Seen On TV)

Buying a property will require a real estate contract or purchase-offer agreement. The contract outlines the "agreement" between the buyer and the seller of the property. Contracts can be very complicated, but it is important for you to understand some basic contract law to ensure you limit your liabilities and also to capitalize on the opportunities available. This section covers the basics of contract law, agreements and offers. If you have specific questions about a contract, call 1-877-IGROWRICH.

A contract or agreement is essentially the agreement of two or more individuals. Not all contracts or agreements need to be in writing. However, a real estate contract must be written. A contract or offer is not legally binding upon the presentation of the contract, but instead when it is accepted in writing, by the other party. Once the agreement is accepted in writing, both individuals are bound by the agreement to the terms and conditions of the contract. The person or entity that made the offer can withdraw the offer at any time prior to acceptance.

In the event the contract or agreement is accepted in writing, the document is the source for the handling of the sale of the property. The individual preparing the transfer of ownership will use the document as the guideline for transfer. The transfer agent may be a title company, banker, or real estate attorney. The agreement will tell the transfer agent how to distribute funds, how to transfer the ownership title, what stays with the property, what goes, and what to do with the outstanding mortgages, and it will indicate the rights of the parties.

There are dozens of real estate contracts and agreements: lease option contracts, option contracts, purchase and sale, sale and purchase, rental agreements, wrap-around mortgages, and many more. You will want to review the various types of contracts and become familiar with their format and text. Also, you can pick up sample contracts at most office supply companies.

The basic information for property transfers is typically covered in standard contract templates available in the marketplace (for example, purchase price, buyer and seller names, location, and financing). However, many transactions require additional conditions and terms. Extra information, conditions, and terms are agreed to by adding another sheet of paper to the contract called an addendum. Often, in the original agreement, contract, or offer, you will see a note that reads "see addendum." The addendum can include a few agreements or many. In addition, it is not uncommon to see an original typed section crossed out (line through the text) with a note stating "see addendum." This allows for contract flexibility so that you can add clauses, terms, and conditions to the document.

Often, you will see the following on an addendum:

"Terms and condition: The terms and conditions of this Addendum prevail in the event of a conflict with the terms and conditions of the attached Agreement of Sale."

In other words, the addendum takes precedence over the contract.

This allows individuals to essentially negate information contained in the original document, changing the conditions and terms. The addendum can be very powerful. A well-written addendum can give you an escape clause, better financing, more rights, less liability, and more negotiation power.

Sections of a Purchase Contract

- **Seller:** The seller's name would be indicated in this section. If the property title is held by more than one party, both names should be included. For example, a husband and wife's names would be included as "John and Mary Smith" as seller.
- **Buyer:** The individual or entity buying the property would have its name here. As a buyer, you may want to include after your name "and/or assigns." This will allow you some additional rights of assignment of the agreement. This guide discusses assignment in greater detail later.
- **Legal Description:** The legal description of the property is not the address, but rather, the legal description as recorded at the courthouse. Typically, it looks something like this "Lot 208, Plan 4539, City of Orlando." If the information is not immediately available, it is common to include in this section "To be supplied at closing" or "legal description to follow." You can typically get the legal description from the courthouse and/or from the homeowner's document of purchase. The closing company can obtain the exact description.
- **Street Address:** The exact address of the property, including street number, street, city, state, and ZIP.

- **Personal Property:** You can ask for any items that are in the property to be included in this section (for example, stoves, refrigerators, washers, dryers, curtains, pool and patio furniture). This is negotiable and normally refers to unattached or detachable property.
- **Purchase Price:** The purchase price of the property.
- **Escrow to be Held:** The funds you deposit as "earnest money" can be held by anyone. Often, the buyer will want to hold the funds, but you can insist on your accountant, a company, or an individual to hold the funds. We recommend the title company or attorney who will be closing the transaction because this is the most convenient.
- **Amount:** The exact amount of money you will deposit with the escrow agent. Obviously you want to make this amount as small as possible so as not to tie up your funds. Again, it is negotiable: $100 to $500 is a standard amount.
- **Promissory Note:** If you need to come up with additional funds to secure the property, you may want to consider a promissory note as an alternative to putting more cash down. The note is an agreement that can be held by an escrow agent. This can be extremely helpful if all parties agree.
- **Assumption of Mortgage:** In this space, indicate the party to assume the mortgage.
- **Interest Rate:** List the interest rate of the mortgage to be assumed.
- **Principal and Interest:** Include the actual amount of the monthly payment that includes the principal and interest

payments. Homeowners should be able to provide this information from their mortgage payment stubs.

- **Approximate Balance:** The balance of the mortgage amount should be listed in this section. Property owners may know the amount, or they may have to contact the mortgage company. The exact amount is not necessary because it will most likely change prior to closing due to the homeowner making additional payments.

- **Money Mortgage:** This is additional financing of the property and may be a third party, or even the seller, financing the property through a mortgage. Spell out the interest rate for the mortgage and the term; try to stay away from balloon payments, which call for a full lump-sum payment.

- **Amount:** Spell out the amount to be financed through a purchase money mortgage.

- **Note "Other":** You do not have to just focus on cash instruments to purchase a property. More than one home has been purchased through trade of goods, services and other property. You would include these other forms of payment in this section.

- **Balance at Close:** Any cash to be transferred to the seller should be specified here. Hopefully, if you have done your negotiation well, this will be "none."

- **Total:** The total should be the same as the purchase price. The payment sections must add up to the purchase price.

See the Contracts and Forms section for examples.

Additional Considerations

- **Interest Rate:** Indicate the maximum interest rate that you would accept. "Prevailing" can be too open-ended and could cause problems. Be specific.
- **Years:** For what period of time (repayment period) shall the note/mortgage be held. Example: 15 years or 30 years.
- **On or Before:** Do not leave your offers open. Set a specific period of time that the offer is valid, after which it is void. Time frames of 24, 48, or 72 hours are not unreasonable. Typically, you would write "on or before January 1, 2013, at 3 p.m." Create a sense of urgency if you can, but realize you can always extend the offer.
- **Closing Day, Month, and Year:** Specify the closing date. Typically, it takes 60 to 90 days to close on a property. Depending on what you want to do with the property, it may be shorter or longer. This date can also be expressed as "on or before."
- **Restrictions, Easements, and Limitations:** If there are any restrictions on the property, they would be identified in this section as "other." Very few cases have restrictions, but they do happen occasionally. The purpose of the property is often "residential."
- **Text:** The balance of the contract/agreement is a template of standard clauses and terms to protect the buyer. Go through the contract and become familiar with the terminology and specific clauses. This sample contract definitely favors the buyer. If you use a seller's contract, realize that the contract may be structured to protect the seller, not you, the buyer. Review contracts in detail. When

it is time to sell the property, you may want to use a different contract, specifically one that tailors to the seller.

- **Acquiring Approvals:** This section specifies the exact nature of the use for the property. It is usually residential, but could be rental or some other objective. It also provides another measure of security to ensure you can get out of the contract if conditions are not met.
- **Special Clauses:** This section is where you may have added additional clauses to the contract. Most of the time you will find "subject to addendum" or "see addendum."
- **Witnesses and Execution:** The buyers' and sellers' signatures must be included to approve the agreement. If there is more than one owner, get *both* signatures. Also, the signature of the escrow agent for the deposit needs to be included (this could be the seller or whoever receives the escrow deposit).
- **Brokerage Fee:** A detailed breakdown and obligation of the brokerage fees to be paid to a broker can be part of the contract (if you are using a broker). Include this paragraph if appropriate.
- **Addendum:** This is your opportunity to add as many clauses to the contract as you would like. Spell out the specifics of the negotiation and agreement in the addendum. Ensure you have escape clauses in case you cannot purchase the property or cannot find another buyer in time. Ask for more concessions.

Potential addendums include:

- Closing costs to be paid per standard contract.

- Contract contingent upon "5-day inspection period"
- Property to be purchased "as is," with no warranties from seller
- Seller to pay $1,000 in collections

Contracts for Purchase and Sale

Risk-Free Contract Clauses

To ensure a risk-free contract, include the following clauses:

- Subject to financial partner's approval (gives you an out)
- And/or assigns (after your name on all contracts to allow you to transfer an agreement)
- Subject to inspection prior to closing (check all properties)
- Deposit five days after acceptance of contract or alternatives
- Subject to mortgages
- Subject to liens being cleared
- Subject to seller Purchase Money Mortgage (PMM) or Owner Take Back (OTB) and fully assumable to the next buyer
- Non-recourse (in case sellers take back mortgage)

Sample Clauses

The deposit check placed with this offer may not be deposited or cashed until all contingencies of this contract have been met to the satisfaction of the buyer and the buyer's associate.

This contract is subject to the approval of the buyer's associate, ____________ (within __ days).

The approval must be in writing and attached to this agreement (within __ days).

This contract is subject to inspection of the property by the buyer's associate, ___________.

This contract is contingent on the buyer or assigns assuming the existing mortgage in favor of ____________________.

- All notes or deeds of trust executed by the buyer shall be non-recourse.
- Subject to inspection of property by buyer and written acceptance of condition of property within ___ days.
- Subject to inspection and acceptance by a qualified person.
- Subject to approval of my (accountant/spouse/ partner/ attorney) (select one).
- Subject to written acceptance by seller within 24 hours.
- Subject to seller purchasing another home.
- Seller to pay one-half of buyer's closing costs.
- Seller to paint the property inside and/or outside.
- Escrow to be transferred to buyer at no charge.
- Seller to pay loan origination points (if any) for buyer's new loan.
- Seller guaranteed all appliances for 90 days from close of sale.
- Seller to pay recording fees.

- Seller to shampoo carpets.
- Seller to leave premises in "move in" condition.
- Seller to do whatever repairs are needed (for example, "patch hole in utility room" or "caulk around tub").
- Seller to leave premises free of all trash and debris.
- Subject to a satisfactory roof, plumbing and electrical inspection to be done within __ days after the date of this contract. Inspection to be paid for by the seller.
- Possession before settlement: "Buyer to receive key to property and right to enter for purposes of physical improvements to property and to show the property to prospective occupants."
- Cash credit to buyer for fix-up work: "Buyer to receive credit at settlement toward down payment for $ ______ for painting, carpeting and general improvements to be made to the property."

Contract Presentation Checklists

Checklist to Use With an Owner or Individual

1. Check contract for accuracy at least twice
2. Check addendum for accuracy at least twice
3. Sign both documents
4. Make copies as required
5. Make presentation to seller
6. Reinforce your position as a real estate investor

a. who closes quickly and pays all closing costs

7. Have all sellers sign agreement and addendum

Checklist to Use With a Realtor

1. Check contract for accuracy at least twice
2. Check addendum for accuracy at least twice
3. Sign both documents
4. Make copies as required
5. Inform Realtor that you will make offer
6. Reinforce your position as a real estate investor
   a. You can close quickly and pay all closing costs
7. Have all sellers sign agreement and addendum

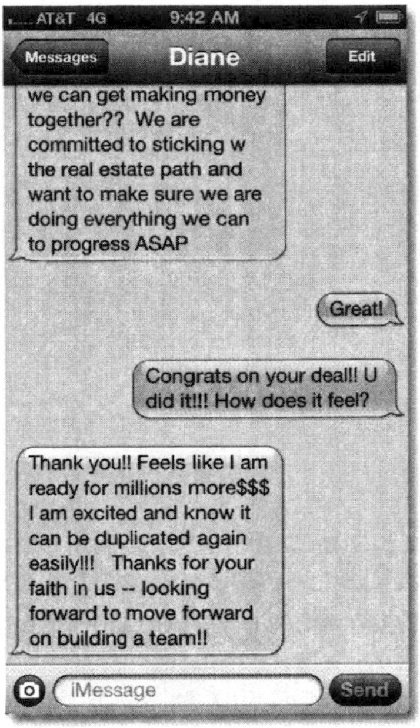
AT&T 4G
9:42 AM
Messages
Diane
Edit
we can get making money together?? We are committed to sticking w the real estate path and want to make sure we are doing everything we can to progress ASAP
Great!
Congrats on your deal!! U did it!!! How does it feel?
Thank you!! Feels like I am ready for millions more$$$ I am excited and know it can be duplicated again easily!!! Thanks for your faith in us -- looking forward to move forward on building a team!!
iMessage
Send

(Case study with Diane)

Chapter 6: Mortgage Financing

Notes and Mortgages (Never Seen On TV)

The purchase of real estate can usually be regarded as a joint venture between an equity investor and a lending institution. Very few occasions arise where properties are bought for all cash. In most real estate transactions, a lender provides part of the financing, and the property is held as security for the debt. There are two instruments involved when a real estate transaction involves *both* debt and equity — the note and the mortgage.

- **Promissory Note:** A promissory note is a signed document acknowledging the existence of a debt and promising repayment. The chief function of the note is to make the borrower personally liable for payment of the debt. Once an individual has signed such a note, the terms of the repayment schedule must be met regardless of the financial success of the document.
- **Mortgage:** A mortgage is a pledge of security for the repayment of the debt. It is created by formal written agreement in which the person who signs a promissory note pledges the property being financed as security (or

collateral) for the debt. Therefore, the mortgage itself is a lien, not evidence of a debt.

Parties to the Mortgage

There are two parties in each mortgage: the mortgagor and the mortgagee. The mortgagor is the borrower, or the one pledging the property as security for the debt incurred. The mortgagee is the lender, or the one to whom the property is pledged.

In the process of borrowing money and pledging property as security, the borrower signs a note, which is *evidence* of the debt. Without this evidence, no mortgage can exist. The mortgage is an instrument that creates an interest in the property. This interest is a lien, or legal claim, on the mortgagor's property until the debt is paid.

Mortgage Requirements

Because a mortgage conveys an interest in real estate, it must be in writing. The actual wording of the document may conform to rather broad guidelines, but should contain essentially the same elements as the deed. The basic mortgage should contain the following elements:

- The mortgagor's (borrower's) legal name must appear. This implies that the mortgagor is of legal age for contracting.
- The mortgagee's (lender's) name must also appear in the mortgage.

- The mortgage must contain words of conveyance or granting from the mortgagor to the mortgagee.
- The instrument must contain a legal description of the mortgaged property that adequately identifies it.
- Reference is usually made to the promissory note, in lieu of the amount of consideration that is found in a typical deed.
- The mortgage must be signed by the mortgagor, although it is not essential for mortgagees to sign the document, they usually do.

Mortgage Theory

In the early years, a mortgage — property pledged to secure a debt — was an actual assignment of that property to a lender. During the period of time that the mortgagor still owed the mortgagee part of the original loan, the lender had physical use of the land and was entitled to any rents or revenue generated from the land. Thus, in earlier forms of mortgages, title to the land pledged as security for a loan was truly transferred to the lender.

Abuses on the part of the lenders brought about more careful wording in mortgage instruments. Slight delays in repaying the loan often resulted in "legal default," with borrowers forfeiting any rights to recovery of title to their land. An outgrowth of the early experiences of both lenders and borrowers is the current-day distinction between the title theory and lien theory of mortgages.

Lien Theory

Lien theory is a more modern approach to creating loan security and is used in most states. In lien theory states, the lender is considered to hold a lien, rather than title, against the property for security of the debt. A lien is the right to have property sold to satisfy a debt. In the event of default on the promissory note, foreclosure procedures are initiated, and the title is conveyed from the borrower to the lender. The mortgage remains with the property until the debt is paid, even if ownership of the property changes.

Title Theory

Fewer than 20 states subscribe to this concept of mortgages. In states with title theory, a mortgage is assumed to represent an actual conveyance of title to the mortgagee, and the document is usually called a "mortgage deed." This can be seen as very similar to the early mortgages in which the mortgagee owned legal title and could take possession or collect revenue from the property during the term of the loan. All of the title theory states have adopted approaches for eliminating abuses in such mortgages.

One alternative is to employ what is called "intermediate title theory." Although this approach requires formal court action to rescind the borrower's legal rights to the property, the mortgagee can assume possession of the property between the time of default and the sheriff's sale. While this system protects the lender against any property, it also protects the mortgagor from eviction without legal process.

Another approach requires that foreclosure proceedings must be held, as in lien theory states. This requirement makes these states' mortgage laws equal in borrower protection to that of lien theory states. The only difference is in the formal wording of the instrument.

Trust Deeds

As mentioned earlier, the typical mortgage involves only two parties, the lender and the borrower. However, in a trust deed, also known as a deed of trust, the borrower conveys the land to a third party. The third party holds the land in trust for the benefit of the holder of the note. The primary reason some states use this form is that the deed of trust can be foreclosed easily and quickly by a trustee's sale under a "power of sale" clause. In prescribed situations, court proceedings may be minimized or eliminated.

Mortgage Clauses

In every mortgage loan, there are several clauses that state the rights of the mortgagor and the mortgagee during the term of the mortgage loan agreement. The various clauses (or provisions) that may be found in the debt agreement are as follows:

- **Acceleration Clause:** Lenders usually insist that the instrument contain an acceleration clause that makes the entire debt due in the event of default. This clause precludes the necessity for the lender to bring separate lawsuits against the same mortgagor for each late payment. This clause usually states that, if any covenants are breached, including the obligation to pay the sums secured by the mortgage when due, then the full amount is due immediately. This declaration of full payment due is at the option of the lender.

- **Cognovit Clause:** This clause is considered to be a confession of judgment. If borrowers allow this clause to be included, they essentially give up their day in court. It authorizes the lender's attorney to obtain a lien judgment against the debtor's real property. Without this clause, the lender must sue on the basis of the note and prove it to be in default.

- **Defeasance Clause:** This clause "defeats" the right of the lender to foreclose on the property as long as the borrower lives up to the terms of the agreement. Thus, as long as the borrower makes periodic payments according to schedule and fulfills all other requirement, the lender may not seize the property or have it sold.

- **Due-on-Sale Clause:** Traditional common law permits a buyer to purchase mortgaged property and preserve the existing mortgage unless the mortgage contains a clause to accelerate the loan upon sale. This due-on-sale clause is especially important to lenders in a world of volatile interest rates. Without it, buyers tend to preserve low-interest mortgages as long as possible by purchasing second mortgage financing rather than refinancing the existing loan.

- **Escalator Clause:** This clause allows the lender to increase the interest rate. Although an escalator clause, in its most general sense, could allow a lender to increase the rate for any reason, it is usually tied to an event or contingency — for example, if it is discovered that the mortgagor is an investor rather than an owner-occupant. Moreover, it could provide for the interest rate to escalate up to the legal maximum in the event of the borrower's default. An escalator clause does not create a variable rate mortgage in which the interest rate is tied to a market index. Escalator clauses in which the interest rate change is at the discretion of the lender are very unpopular with borrowers. The potential for abuse and unfavorable public relations far outweigh any benefits.

- **Exculpatory Clause:** An exculpatory clause relieves the borrower of personal liability to repay the loan. Thus, if the borrower defaults, the lender can look only to the property foreclosure for recovery of the debt. In effect, the lender may not sue the borrower on the note or obtain a deficiency judgment if the sale of the property at foreclosure does not provide sufficient funds to cover the loan's balance. Obviously, borrowers prefer to negotiate loans with exculpatory clauses, but lenders are usually willing to allow them.

- **Open-End Clause:** Many institutions (particularly savings and loans) write loan agreements that allow a borrower to increase the amount of a loan after the loan balance has been paid down. The loan can usually be increased to the original amount borrowed. While closing costs and loan fees are avoided by using an open-end provision, the lender usually reserves the right to adjust the interest rate if the current market rate is higher than the rate on the loan being opened.

- **Prepayment Clause:** To prepay means to pay off the indebtedness before the end of the loan term. Under traditional common law, the mortgagor has no right to prepay a mortgagor unless the right is explicitly provided by a prepayment clause. In some states, statutory law has reversed this. Now, any note that is silent as to the right of the borrower to prepay the note in advance of the stated maturity date may be prepaid in full by the borrower (or successor) in interest without penalty. In typical prepayment clauses, a statement is made as to (1) whether there is a penalty for prepayment, (2) whether extra payments directly reduce the principal upon which interest is computed or eliminates the last payment, and (3) whether the number and size of extra payments in any one year are restricted. Some lenders try to discourage a fast turnover of funds, which is costly to them, by imposing prepayment penalties during the early years. These penalties are usually stated as a percentage of the unpaid balance, and the percentage charged is usually reduced in later years of the mortgage term. Most savings and loans institutions have a prepayment clause in the note. Typically, it states that the borrower has the right to prepay the outstanding principal amount in whole or in part and that the outstanding amount of the extra payment is applied against the principal amount. In addition, such clauses usually state that any extra payment does not extend or postpone the due date of subsequent monthly installments, or change the amount of the installments.

- **Redemption Clause:** Prior to foreclosure, a borrower has the right to pay the amount owed, plus interest, in order to retain the property or interest in the property. This right is called the equity of redemption and is a matter of law, not negotiation. Nevertheless, the right is stated in most mortgages.

- **Release Clause:** An acquisition and development loan obtained by a developer may be used to develop a number of building lots. Many such loan agreements contain clauses that allow the developer to release developed lots as security for the loan. In addition, a specified amount is paid back to the lender. Usually the amount that must be paid to obtain the release is greater than the proportionate amount of the loan allocated to the lot. For example, if a developer borrows $100,000 to develop 10 lots, the release amount might be $12,000 per lot — $2,000 more than the amount loaned per lot.

- **Renegotiable Rate Clause:** A renegotiable rate mortgage (RRM) is a series of short-term loans secured by a long-term mortgage. The short-term loans are automatically renewable at equal intervals of three to five years each. The mortgage terms may not exceed 40 years. The monthly payments are made in equal installments. However, at the end of the life of each short-term loan, the interest rate may be changed. Changes are based on the movement of an index such as the Federal Home Loan Bank Board's most recent monthly National Average Contract Mortgage Rate index. The interest rate is the only term that may be altered. An interest rate modification results in a change of the monthly payment. The new payment amount remains stable until the loan term has again expired.

- **Subordination Clause:** A lien-holder may consent to place his or her interest in a property at a lower priority than another lien-holder through the use of a subordination clause. A subordination clause is often used when the seller of vacant land takes back a purchase money mortgage. In order to make the sale, the seller agrees to lower the priority of the lien to a position inferior to a construction or permanent loan. Sometimes landowners who lease their land will also subordinate their fee position to a construction *or* permanent loan obtained by the lessee.

- **Variable Rate Clause:** The variable rate mortgage (VRM) ties the interest to some specified index of market interest rates. As the market fluctuates, either the periodic (usually monthly) payment or the loan's maturity would increase or decrease depending on whether the rate went up or down. Until 1980, federally chartered savings and loans were precluded from increasing a loan's monthly payments. However, financial deregulation during the early 1980s freed S&Ls from such restrictions, and they can now make many types of loans in which periodic payments may vary.

  The clauses discussed in this section are the principal variable provisions found in mortgages or notes. Other provisions that are sometimes used include equity participation and late payment clauses. Depending on the type of lender, each will usually have a standard form that outlines the rights of the lender and the borrower. All borrowers should carefully read these documents before signing. They may contain a clause that is detrimental to their particular needs.

  Fortunately for home mortgages, the influence of secondary mortgage market agencies has in recent years encouraged the widespread use of a standard home mortgage contract. This document, promulgated by the Federal Home Loan Mortgage Corporation (FHLMC) and the Federal National Mortgage Association (FNMA), is well-crafted to protect the interests of both mortgagor and mortgagee.

Types of Mortgages

Mortgages may be classified according to several criteria — depending on (1) whether or not they are underwritten by an agency of the U.S. government, (2) the method of payment, (3) the priority of the lien or (4) the purpose of payment for which they were made. The classifications are not mutually exclusive. For example, a package mortgage could be either conventional or government underwritten. Similarly, a participation mortgage could be either fully or partially amortized. Thus, the classifications are simply different ways of looking at the same mortgage.

Government Underwritten vs. Conventional Mortgages

Government underwritten loans are insured or guaranteed by an agency of the U.S. government. The Federal Housing Administration insures loans made by private lenders to qualified buyers of properties that meet minimum standards. The Veterans Affairs guarantees loans made by such lenders to veterans. A 1% user fee is charged by the VA for a guarantee. The FHA charges a premium for loan insurance, as described below.

FHA-Insured Mortgages

The Federal Housing Administration was created under the National Housing Act of 1934. Under this act, the FHA was granted the authority to insure mortgage loans made by private lenders. It is important to understand that the FHA issues an insurance policy, whose premiums are paid by the borrower, which guarantees that the lenders will receive their money in the event the mortgagors fail to make their payments.

There are several types of FHA mortgage programs, including low-income housing, nursing homes, cooperative apartments and condominium apartments. The most common FHA program is for single-family homes as authorized by Title 11,

Section 203, of the National Housing Act. Under this program, the borrower pays a one-time insurance premium based on several factors. The premiums may be financed over the life of the loan if the seller pays the closing costs. The premiums for FHA insurance are deposited in the Mutual Mortgage Insurance Fund. The FHA reimburses a lender from this fund if a borrower defaults, the mortgagor's interest is foreclosed, and the Secretary of Housing and Urban Development (HUD) takes title to the property. The FHA must then sell the property.

Lenders will generally loan a higher percentage of the appraised value with an insured mortgage. There may be times when a potential homebuyer does not have a sufficient down payment to qualify for a conventional loan. In this case, an FHA-insured mortgage may be appropriate. However, the insurance premium is an added expense to the borrower.

VA-Guaranteed Mortgages

The U.S. Department of Veterans Affairs (formerly the Veterans Administration) was created just after World War II as part of the Servicemen's Readjustment Act and was authorized to guarantee a stated percentage of loans made to qualified veterans by qualified lenders.

Although the VA does not normally make loans in areas where there are no lending institutions, the VA will grant loans directly to veterans. Generally, the VA guarantees loans that are made by lending institutions to veterans. When a borrower defaults, the VA will pay up to 50% of the amount of the loan where the loan is $45,000 or less. For larger loans, the VA will pay any loss up to a maximum of $22,500 plus 40 cents per additional dollar of the loan over $45,000, up to a total loss limit of $36,000. Because VA loans are available up to 100% of the selling price, brokers are able to sell homes to veterans who otherwise could not afford to purchase a home. In this case, a veteran is entitled to only one VA loan; however, in some cases, the loan can be transferred to another eligible veteran, and the original borrower's right to a loan is restored.

Conventional Mortgages

In recent years, the percentage of FHA and VA mortgages has been decreasing. The majority of mortgages today are conventional. Conventional loans are preferred by lenders for two reasons. First, lenders have the flexibility to create loans that reflect their own requirements. This permits individualized programs that are in the best interest of both parties. Second, more paperwork and red tape are required for loans that are guaranteed or insured, and administrative costs are higher.

Generally, a conventional mortgage requires a larger down payment than an FHA or VA mortgage. In the VA program, the borrower is not allowed to pay points on a new loan. However, the borrower may be required to pay points when refinancing or rolling over. (Points are a discount from the face amount of the loan, which increases the yield to the lender). In conventional and FHA mortgages, borrowers are allowed to, and in many cases do, pay loan fees, user fees, or discount points.

Mortgages by Method of Payment

Standard Fixed-Payment Mortgage

A standard fixed-payment mortgage (SFPM) is a fully amortized loan that is completely paid off by equal, periodic payments. This is the standard type of loan used to finance single-family homes today. It is also used sometimes for income-producing properties, although partially amortized loans are used more frequently to finance these properties. Payments on fully amortized mortgages are usually required monthly. At maturity of the loan, the loan balance is zero.

Straight (or Straight-Term) Mortgage

A loan in which only interest payments are made periodically and a final payment of principal is made at the end of the term is called a straight (or straight-term) loan. Although such loans are not used frequently to finance the purchase of single-family houses, they are used quite often in land transactions. In these situations, developers will be able to pay for the land after development and sale. In the interim, they pay interest only.

Partially Amortized Mortgage

If a loan is not completely paid off by equal, periodic payments, but periodic payments are required, it is a partially amortized loan. In other words, the loan will be partially paid off by periodic payments, but there will be a remaining balance on the loan that must be paid off at maturity. This remaining balance on a partially amortized loan is called a balloon and is satisfied by a balloon payment.

Mortgages by Payment or Yield Variability (AMLs, GPMs and SAMS)

Adjustable Mortgage Loan (AML)

In 1981, the Federal Home Loan Bank Board issued regulations incorporating both variable and renegotiable rate mortgages into adjustable mortgage loan regulations. "An adjustable mortgage loan permits adjustment of the interest rate, which may be implemented through changes in the payment amount, the outstanding principal loan balance, the loan term, or any combination of these variables" (source: FHLBB Res. No. 8-12069 1981). As with VRMs and RRMs, interest rates must be decreased as the index decreases and, of course, may be increased as the index rises. The lender may increase the loan term up to 40 years to cover interest-rate increases (although such an extension comes at the discretion of the lender, not the borrower).

The interest rate may be tied to any index beyond the control of the lender and may be adjusted as often as monthly. Examples of indexes to which an AML may be tied are:

- The FHLB district cost of funds to Federal Savings and Loan Insurance Corporation (FSLIC)-insured savings and loans.
- The National Average Contract Mortgage Rate for the purchase of existing homes.
- The monthly average of weekly auction rates on three-month or six-month U.S. Treasury bills.
- The monthly average yield on U.S. Treasury securities adjusted to constant maturities of one, two, three, or five years. All of these indexes are published in the Federal Reserve Bulletin.

Notice of interest rate changes must be given to borrowers at least 30 days, but no more than 45 days, prior to the change. Lenders may not charge a prepayment penalty or fee associated with interest-rate changes.

Within these regulations and guidelines, lenders may establish their own AML plans. However, administrative costs, competition, and secondary market requirements limit flexibility for most lenders in this regard.

Frequent adjustments are costly. Competitors may limit the frequency and magnitude of adjustments. And secondary market lenders have established certain limitations for the AMLs they will purchase. For example, the Federal Housing Loan Mortgage Corporation will not purchase AMLs that allow rising balances or that have a subsidized payment (or "buy down") in the early months.

Graduated Payment Mortgage

In a graduated payment mortgage (GPM), the payments begin at a lower level than in a comparable standard fixed-payment mortgage. They gradually rise to an amount greater than the payment in the standard fixed-payment mortgage. After the period for payment increases ends, the payments for the remaining term are fixed.

In the early years of a GPM loan, interest accrues at a higher rate than is actually paid. The unpaid interest is added to the principal balance. This is called negative amortization because the remaining balance is increasing rather than decreasing.

There are several plans for FHA-insured GPMs under Section 245 of the National Housing Act. The approved plans are:

- Plan I: Payments rise 2.5% annually for 5 years.
- Plan II: Payments rise 5% annually for 5 years.
- Plan III: Payments rise 7.5% annually for 5 years.
- Plan IV: Payments rise 2% annually for 10 years.
- Plan V: Payments rise 3% annually for 10 years.

Shared Appreciation Mortgage

A shared appreciation mortgage (SAM) allows a lender to charge a below-market periodic interest rate by sharing in the property's sale proceeds at time of sale or upon maturity of the loan. The payment to the lender upon maturity or sale is termed "contingent deferred interest." The percentage share of the property's appreciation the lender will receive is established in the loan agreement.

While there have been numerous advocates of SAM home loans, no large-scale program has been implemented. One cause of this is that home appreciation is geographically correlated with income and ethnic/racial characteristics; therefore, the loan could be inherently discriminatory. A second cause is that typical terms do not return a competitive yield to lenders. In income property lending, however, the SAM idea is used as one form of a "participation" mortgage loan.

Mortgages by Purpose

Mortgage forms vary in their payback provisions, terms of agreement, and types of property used as security. Some are created to achieve specific purposes or to fit the need of the individual borrower. The types of mortgages classified according to purpose are as follows:

Purchase Money Mortgage

The distinguishing characteristic of a purchase money mortgage is that the title and the mortgage are conveyed in the same transaction. The loan involved could be from a third party, and it could be a first mortgage loan. However, typically, the purchase money mortgage is a second mortgage given by the seller to the buyer to partially finance the purchase through installment payments.

Purchase money mortgages are common in all types of real estate purchases. In the purchases of raw land in large quantities by a developer, the landowner may accept a partial cash payment and take a mortgage for the remainder of the selling price. As the developer sells lots from the completed subdivision, the mortgage is paid off. In effect, the landowner is a partner with the developer through the use of a purchase money mortgage.

Purchase money mortgages are also common in transactions involving residential properties, such as when the buyer does not have a sufficient down payment. The remainder may be obtained by assuming an existing mortgage or by giving the seller a new mortgage. Either way, the seller is willing to take a mortgage as part of the payment.

Consider the following example to illustrate the use of a purchase money mortgage in residential properties. Seller A is asking $80,000 for a single-family residence. Buyer B wants the house but only has $10,000 for a down payment. The lending institution will only loan $64,000 on the house. To be able to sell the house, Seller A agrees to take a purchase money mortgage for $6,000 from Buyer B. In addition to taking this purchase money mortgage, Seller A is willing to accept a lower priority of claim if Buyer B should default. In this case, the lending institution has the first claim because it has a first mortgage. The purchase money mortgage is a second mortgage.

Participation Mortgage

A participation mortgage is a loan agreement that enables the lender to receive part of the income from an investment in addition to the interest payments. Participation mortgages became popular during periods of high interest rates and are used by lenders to increase their yields. The participation feature enables them to share in the expected success of income-producing properties. It also protects the borrower from abnormally high payments if income projections are not realized. The participation can be a specified percentage of gross or net income, a share of proceeds at sale, or both.

The use of a closely related term, mortgage participation, occurs when two or more lending institutions combine their funds to finance a real estate project. For example, a lender does not want the risk of a project that is the magnitude for which an investor is seeking a loan. In this case, the "primary" lender may call upon another lender to "participate" in this loan, thereby creating a participation. For example, an investor needs $100 million to purchase a large hotel complex. The lending institution to which the developer applies for a loan may not be able to lend that much money. By obtaining one or more "participants," the original lender is able to obtain the money needed for the investor. In return, all lenders receive evidence of debt from the borrower, as well as an instrument pledging the property as security for each lender's note.

Blanket Mortgage

A blanket mortgage covers more than one parcel of land. Developers of subdivisions employ this type of mortgage, which permits small portions of the land (residential lots) to be paid off and released from the mortgage. This clause is known as a release clause because the remainder of the land continues to be held as security for the loan. The percentage of the original mortgage that is released is usually smaller than the pro-rated dollar amount. For example, the developer has a note for $100,000 on a subdivision with 20 lots. The lender will usually require more than 1/20th of the mortgage dollar amount to be paid before releasing a lot from the mortgage.

Reverse Annuity Mortgage

The reverse annuity mortgage (RAM) was conceived as a way to enable older homeowners to liquidate and consume the equity "locked up" in their home. As the name suggests, in its simplest form, the homeowner would receive a regular disbursement from the lender, secured by a mortgage. The regular disbursements and interest accruing against them accumulate eventually to some maximum loan balance.

The major problem with this simple RAM is that the homeowner may outlive the time when the maximum loan is reached. While various solutions to this risk are being explored, there is yet to be a significant use of the RAM in the United States. Prudence requires that the loan be made to a homeowner late in life, and for a fairly small percentage of the property's value.

Package Mortgage

A package mortgage allows homebuyers to pledge household items of personal property, in addition to the real estate, as security for a loan. For instance, lending institutions may allow items such as ranges, refrigerators, dishwashers or air conditioners to serve as security, thereby allowing the homebuyer to finance major appliances over the term of the loan at relatively low mortgage interest rates. This practice allows lenders to increase the amount of a loan with no added administrative costs and little additional risk. It allows buyers to purchase home appliances and other major items of equipment they may otherwise not be able to afford.

Home Equity Loan/Equity Line of Credit

By far the fastest growing type of mortgage loan in recent years has been the home equity loan or equity line of credit. It is a second mortgage loan that permits any number of draws or balance reductions, subject to a maximum of 75% to 80% of house value, including the first mortgage loan. The monthly payment typically is the greater of a fixed percentage of the current balance, usually 1% or 2%, or a modest dollar minimum. The interest rate is variable, usually prime (or another short-term interest rate) plus 1.5% to 2%. Draws against the mortgage usually are by check, though in some cases, credit cards access the equity credit line.

Mortgages by Lien Priority

- **First Mortgage:** A first mortgage is the mortgage instrument that creates the first lien on a property. As explained in the Purchase Money Mortgage section, the holder of the note secured by the first mortgage will have its claims satisfied before any subsequent mortgagees.
- **Junior Mortgage:** Any mortgage that is not a first mortgage is "junior" to the first mortgage. This means that, in case of default, the claims of the holder of a note secured by a second mortgage or lower-priority mortgage will not be satisfied until the first mortgage is satisfied. Because of the subordinated nature of these mortgages, they carry a higher level of risk. With the addition of greater risk, lenders generally charge a higher interest rate.

Mortgaged Property Transfers

In the transfer of mortgaged property, two situations typically arise: (1) the mortgagor sells the property, or (2) the mortgagee sells the mortgage. When the mortgagor sells the property, the buyer may take the property "subject to" the mortgage, or the buyer may "assume" the mortgage. When the mortgagee sells its mortgage interest, the sale must be by "assignment."

Transfers Subject to Mortgage

When a buyer obtains property subject to a mortgage, the buyer realizes the existence of the mortgage. As long as the buyer makes the mortgage payments, no problems arise. Suppose, however, that the buyer defaults. The seller is still liable for the debt and may elect to make the payments. If the seller does not make the payments, however, the lender will foreclose, and the property will be sold. If the sale price is not adequate to pay off the debt, the seller, not the buyer, is liable for the deficiency.

Mortgage Assumptions

When a buyer assumes a mortgage, the buyer covenants and promises to pay any deficit that might occur from a subsequent default. Therefore, if the buyer goes into default, and after the foreclosure sale, money is still owed on the debt, then both the buyer and the seller may be held responsible for the deficit.

Mortgage Assignments

A mortgage assignment occurs when a mortgagee sells a mortgage. The assignment is a brief form stating that the mortgagee — the assignor — transfers and assigns the mortgage and mortgage note to the purchaser — the assignee. Prior to the assignment, the assignee should give the mortgagor written notice of the assignment. The assignee should also, prior to the assignment, obtain a certificate of estoppel from the mortgagor. The certificate of estoppel is a written document that states the balance due on the debt and all defenses or claims against the mortgagee.

Default and Foreclosure

Default

Default is defined as the nonperformance of a duty or obligation, whether arising under a contract or otherwise, such as the failure to make payment called for by a note. Default can also occur if the mortgagor fails to pay taxes, insurance premiums or otherwise breaches any of the covenants in the mortgage instrument.

Default does not necessarily lead to foreclosure. After default occurs, lenders usually try to avoid foreclosing. Foreclosure action usually arises only after default has occurred and after the mortgagee decides there is no hope of collecting the amount owed through normal negotiation with the borrower.

Foreclosure/Public Sale

If a borrower defaults on a secured loan, the mortgagee must bring foreclosure action to eliminate the mortgagor's interest in the property. In most states, the preferred method of foreclosure is by public sale. The proceeds of the sale are then applied to the indebtedness. When the property sells for more than the debt, the mortgagor receives the balance, saving at least some of the investment.

Foreclosure/Deficiency Judgment

When a foreclosed property sells for less than the debt, the mortgagee must look to the note for the remainder of the debt. To do this, the mortgagee first obtains a deficiency judgment against the signatories to the note and then attempts to collect against their personal assets.

- **Junior Lien-holders:** When foreclosure begins, all junior lien-holders should join in the suit. If the property sells for less than the debt, the junior lien-holders can sue the mortgagor on the note. If the property sells for more than the debt, the junior lien-holders are paid off out of the surplus in order of their priority, with the mortgagor receiving the balance. The purchaser of the property then receives the property free and clear of the first lien (which was foreclosed) and all liens junior to it. The only exception to this involves real estate taxes. All real estate tax liens must be paid from the foreclosure sale, or the property passed to the purchaser is subject to all unpaid taxes. The purchaser must then pay the remaining taxes due or lose the property.
- **Soldiers and Sailors Relief Act:** The Soldiers and Sailors Relief Act affects mortgages in several ways. One provision states that the court in which the foreclosure appears has the right to stop proceedings in which a civilian mortgagor, after induction to the military, is unable

to comply with the mortgage agreement. For example, a mortgagor might be unable to meet the payments because of a reduction of income after entering the military. Another provision states that the mortgagee can collect a maximum of 6% interest while the mortgagor is in the military, unless the mortgagor's ability to pay is not affected by military status.

(Vacant homes are all over, just look)

Chapter 7: Investor Contacts & Groups

Investor Directory (Never Seen On TV)
This directory, was created with the intention of you having access to when, where, and what real estate events are taking place, in or near by your city. Imagine access to every active and serious investor at your fingertips. If you market, advertise, or promote opportunities to each association or club any good deal you have to offer, can be placed nationally. Reach out for partners, for whatever reason you find one could be used.

We bring you the list of all many active groups and associations that promote real estate and the wealth generated from the business. Use this directory!

ALABAMA

Associated Investors of Alabama
Homewood, AL.
205-871-5284
www.aiaclub.com

Mobile Real Estate Investment Group
Mobile, AL.
251-366-4663
www.mobile-rig.com

North Alabama Real Estate Investors Assoc.
Florence, AL.
205-828-0502

Real Estate Navigators of Huntsville
Huntsville, AL.
256-755-2099
www.hsvlnavigators.com

Tuscaloosa Real Estate Investor's Assoc.
Tuscaloosa, AL.
205-366-0411

ALASKA

Alaska Assoc. of Realtors
www.alsakrealtors.com

Alaska REIA
907-248-7088
www.ak-reia.com

Alaska Property Owners Assoc.
Anchorage, AK.
907-333-1244

ARIZONA

Arizona Prosperity Investment Group

Phoenix, AZ.
480-539-7900
www.azpig.com

Arizona Real Estate Investors Assoc.
Phoenix, AZ.
480-990-7092
www.azreia.org

Phoenix Real Estate Club
Phoenix, AZ.
480-990-7092 (same as AZREIA)
www.phoenixrealestateclub.com

Scottsdale Investor Real Estate Group
Chandler, AZ.
602-625-2225

Talisman of Tucson's Real Estate Investors United
Tucson, Arizona
520-940-5488
www.treiu.com

ARKANSAS

Northwest Arkansas Real Estate Investors Assoc.
Rogers, Arkansas
479-531-7330
www.uscentralreia.com

CALIFORNIA

American Investors Club of Malibu
Malibu, CA.

310-497-1510

Autumn Leaf Real Estate Investment Club
Temecula, CA.
951-693-5870
www.alreoc.com

Bay Area Investors Resource Center
Burlingame, CA.
650-508-1195
www.irca-sanfrancisco.com

Bay Area Wealth Builders Assoc.
Mill Valley, CA.
707-996-6411
www.bawb.info

Capital City Wealth Builders
Sacramento, CA.
800-650-1315
www.ccwealthbuilders.com

Directed Real Estate Professionals
Glendale, CA.

East Bay Wealth Builders Club
San Ramon, CA.
866-235-9264
www.eastbaywealthbuilders.com

Elk Grove REI Group
Elk Grove, CA.
916-416-5510
www.elkgroverei.com

Financial Enlightenment Club
Santa Rosa, CA.
888-851-3367 ext. 703
www.financialenlightenmentclub.com

Invest Club for Women
Irvine, CA.
714-904-0080
www.womensinvestclub.com

Investing in Real Estate Clubs
Beverly Hills, CA.
Duarte, CA.
Glendale, CA.
Fontana, CA.
Long Beach, CA.
Manhattan Beach, CA.
Canooga Park, CA.
877-285-8669
www.investinginrealestateclubs.com

Investors Workshops
Orange, CA.
714-389-0919
www.investorsworkshops.com

Investors Workshops
Sacramento, CA.
916-223-5564
www.investorsworkshopsnorth.com

Mid Peninsula Real Estate Investors Club
Foster City, CA.
408-264-3198

www.sjrei.com

Monterey Bay Investment Club
Monterey, California
408-264-3198
www.mbreic.com

Monterey Bay Real Estate Investors Club
Seaside, CA.
408-264-3198
www.sjrei.com

National Real Estate Investment Club
Pleasanton, California
925-846-2582
www.nreiclub.com

New Real Estate Investors Club
Yuba City, CA.
Chico, CA.
530-846-7200
www.nreic-ca.com

North San Diego Real Estate Investors Assoc.
Vista, CA.
760-809-4666
www.nsdrei.org

Orange County Real Estate Forum
Irvine, CA.
949-726-8446
www.ocreforum.com

Prosper Real Estate Investment Club of Santa Barbara
Santa Barbara, CA.
866-702-5188
www.prosperreia.com

Real Estate Investment Club of Santa Barbara
Santa Barbara, CA.
805-898-9177

Real Estate Investors Club of America
Burlingame, CA.
916-941-9977 ext. 260
www.nreclubs.com

Real Estate Investors Assoc.
Apple Valley, CA.
702-735-6000
www.realestateinvestorsassociation.org

Real Estate Investors Club of Los Angeles
Culver City, CA.
310-793-7069
www.realestateclub-la.com

Real Estate Wealth Network
Hermosa Beach, CA.
310-937-6927
www.rewealthnetwork.com

Real Wealth Network
Sacramento, CA.
877-700-9325
www.realwealthnetwork.com

Roseville REI Club
Roseville, CA.
916-612-7741
www.rreic.com

SIS International Real Estate Club
San Bernardino, CA.
909-648-3537
www.sisinternationalinvestmentclub.com

Sacramento Real Estate Investment Assoc.
Sacramento, CA.
916-481-6607
www.sacreia.com

Sacramento Valley Real Estate Investment Club
Rocklin, CA.
916-791-3032
www.svreic.com

San Diego Creative Real Estate Investors Assoc.
San Diego, CA.
www.sdcia.com

San Jose Real Estate Investors Club
Santa Clara, CA.
408-264-3198
www.sjrei.net

Silicon Valley Investment Club
San Jose, CA.
408-515-1122
www.sviclub.com

SOCAL Creative Investors Assoc.
La Jolla, CA.
857-756-9204
www.socalcia.com

Southern California REIC
Torrance, CA.
310-592-4045

Real Estate Investors Network
Studio City, CA.
Westlake Village, CA.
805-267-1173
www.reinclub.com

VLD Realty Club
Sacramento, CA
916-419—0500 ext. 172
www.hardmonayinvesting.net

Your Real Estate Club
Brea, CA.
951-347-6027
www.yourreclub.com

COLORADO

Boulder County Real Estate Investors
Longmont, CO.
720-318-5445
www.bcrei.com

Colorado Assoc. of Real Estate Investors
Colorado Springs, CO.

800-665-7051
www.csrec.com

Colorado Assoc. of Real Estate Investors
South Aurora, CO.
303-398-7035
www.carei.com

Front Range Assoc. of Real Estate Investors
Colorado Springs, CO.
719-649-6318
www.frarei.com

Investors of Northern Colorado
Windsor, CO.
800-767-5085 ext. 600
www.theincclink.com

Investors Resource Realty of Colorado
Greenwood Village, CO.
303-805-5570
www.irrofcolorado.com

Northern Colorado Creative Investors Club
Greeley, CO.
970-481-0525

Springs Real Estate Investors Network
Colorado Springs, CO.
719-638-6651
www.srein.com

Western Slope Real Estate Investors
Grand Junction, CO.

970-261-5450
www.wsrei.com

CONNECTICUT

Connecticut Real Estate Investor's & Apartment Owners Assoc.
Cromwell, CT.
860-561-8821
www.ctreia.com

DELAWARE

Money Answers
610-447-0342

FLORIDA

2x4 Investor Network
Port Saint Lucie, FL.
772-232-9308

Boca Real Estate Investment Club
954-427-7700
www.bocarealestate.net

Bradenton Real Estate Club
Bradenton, FL.
941-746-0505
www.bradentonrealestateclub.com

Broward County Landlords Assoc.
Fort Lauderdale, FL.
954-753-6052

www.browardlandlords.com

Broward Real Estate Investors Assoc.
Davie, FL.
888-839-2444
www.breia.com

Central Florida Landlords
Kissimmee, FL.
407-892-5836
www.centralfloridalandlord.com

Central Florida Realty Investors Assoc.
Orlando, FL.
407-328-7773
www.cfri.net

Florida Homebuyers Alliance
Oakland Park, FL.
954-491-4321

Florida Investor's Assoc.
Stuart, FL.
772-403-5811
www.thefina.com

Florida Landlord Network
Jacksonville, FL.
904-387-3122
www.flalandlord.com

Florida Real Estate Investors Assoc.
West Palm Beach, FL.
561-819-5686

www.flreia.com

Gator Real Estate Investors Assoc.
Gainesville, FL.
864-578-3553
www.gatorreia.com

Investor Resource Center
Winter Park/Orlando, FL.
407-831-2498

Jacksonville Real Estate Investors Assoc.
Jacksonville, FL.
904-448-4467
www.jaxreia.com

Miami Real Estate Investors Assoc.
Miami, FL.
305-303-5173
www.investmentpropertiesmiamiflorida.com

Millionaires Real Estate Investment Club
Fort Lauderdale, FL.
561-706-7053
www.millionairesclubonline.com

Monday Night Investors
St. Petersburg, FL.
727-420-4810

North Florida Real Estate Investors Assoc.
Tallahassee, FL.
850-212-6191
www.nfreia.com

Pensacola Real Estate Navigators
Pensacola, FL.
850-505-4111
www.renavigators.com

Polk County Real Estate Investors Assoc.
Lakeland, FL.
863-640-4968
www.pcreia.com

Polk County Real Estate Networking Assoc.
Lakeland, FL.
863-683-4482

Port Charlotte Real Estate Investors Assoc.
Port Charlotte, FL.
941-726-4162

Real Estate Investors Network
Margate, FL.
954-563-8521
www.reinvestorsnetwork.com

Sarasota Real Estate Investors Assoc.
Sarasota, FL.
941-927-0040
www.sarasotareia.com

Southwest Florida Real Estate Investors Assoc.
Fort Meyers. FL.
800-605-2910 ext. 120
www.swflreia.com

Sun Coast Real Estate Investors Assoc.
Tampa, FL.
813-882-3170
www.sreia.com

Tampa Bay Real Estate Investors Assoc.
Clearwater, FL.
813-404-7639
www.tbreia.com

Lighthouse Assoc. of Landlords
Altamonte Springs, FL.
407-772-0853
www.lighthouselandlords.org

Polk County Real Estate Investors Assoc.
863-683-0073
www.pfahi.com

Real Estate Investors Network of NE Florida
Jacksonville, FL.
904-378-8092
www.rein-jax.com

Treasure Coast Real Estate Investors Assoc.
St. Lucie West, FL.
772-343-7338
www.tcreia.com

Urban Real Estate Investors Assoc.
Miami, FL.
305-479-2403

Wealth Builders Real Estate Investors Assoc.
Tampa, FL.
800-335-0256
www.reea.com

Wealth In Real Estate
Jacksonville, FL.
904-389-8800
www.jaxwire.com

Ma & Pa Landlord Assoc.
Fort Lauderdale, FL.
954-527-5182

Young Entrepreneurs Society
Sarasota, FL.
941-927-5646
www.yes941.com

GEORGIA

Investors Resource Center
Dunwoody, GA.
678-999-3896
www.reiatl.com

Macon Middle Georgia Real Estate Investors Assoc.
Macon, GA.
478-955-2321
www.gareia.org

Macon Real Estate Investment Assoc.
Macon, GA.
478-993-6082

www.maconreia.com

North Metro Real Estate Investors Assoc.
Acworth, GA.
770-573-2143
www.northmetroreia.com

Columbus Real Estate Investors Group
706-561-5301

HAWAII

Hawaii Real Estate Investors
Honolulu, HI.
808-368-6548
www.hirei.org

Hawaii Property Center
808-328-9595

Maui Real Estate Investment Club
Kahului, HI
808-573-2219

IDAHO

Boise REIA
Boise, ID.
208-866-4041

Exit Strategies Inc.
Boise, ID.
801-302-8524

Idaho Investor Group
Pocatello, ID.
208-234-0550
www.idahoinvestor.com

Mastermind Real Estate Club of SE Idaho
Idaho Falls, ID.
208-680-4138

Millionaire Real Estate Investor
Coeur d' Alene, ID.
208-699-5348

Treasure Valley Real Estate Investment Club
Nampa, ID.
208-429-9000

ILLINOIS

Angel Real Estate Investing
708-839-6372

Central Illinois Investors Assoc.
Morton, IL.
309-545-0009
www.ciia.us

Chicago Area Real Estate Investors Assoc.
Glendale Heights, IL.
630-942-9500
www.careia.org

Chicago Creative Investors Assoc.
Glen Ellyn, IL.

618-877-6352
www.mela-il.com

Metro East Landlords Assoc.
Collinsville, IL.
618-877-MELA

Midwest Real Estate Assoc. of Chicago
Elgin, IL.
847-741-9797
www.midwestrea.com

Northern Illinois Real Estate Assoc.
Johnsburg, IL.
815-363-0233
www.northernilrea.com

RA Chicago Investors Group
Elmhurst, IL.
630-883-4210
www.thequeenofshortsales.com

Lake County Apartment Owners Assoc.
847-855-5974

Ben Franklin Investment Club
773-731-8010

Freeport Area Landlord Assoc.
815-233-4663

Illinois Rental Property Owners Assoc.
630-415-0543
www.irpoa.org

South Suburban Real Estate Investors
Chicago Heights, IL.
708-572-0200
www.ssrei.org

INDIANA

Apartment Assoc. of East Central Indiana
Muncie, IN.
765-288-2492
www.rentmuncie.com

Central Indiana Real Estate Investors Assoc.
Indianapolis, IN.
317-514-0009
www.cireia.org

Indianapolis Landlord Assoc.
317-571-1246

Indy Property Investors
Indianapolis, IN.
317-788-0386

Northwest Indiana Real Estate Investors Assoc.
Hammond, IN.
219-937-6697

Michiana Income Property Owners Assoc.
South Bend, IN.
574-235-3634
www.mipoa.com

Shelby County Property Investors
Shelbyville, IN.
317-398-3333
IOWA

Two Rivers Real Estate Investors Assoc.
Des Moines, IA.
515-710-1955
www.tworiversreia.org

KANSAS

Kansas City Investment Group
Shawnee, KS.
816-292-2822
www.kcig.org

Partners for Responsible Neighborhoods
316-267-6560

Landlords of Johnson County
Overland Park, KS.
913-236-5334
www.jocolandlords.org

KENTUCKY

Bluegrass Real Estate Investment Assoc.
Lexington, KY.
859-278-0388
www.bluegrassreia.com

Kentuckian Real Estate Investors Assoc.
Louisville, KY.

502-326-0074
www.kreia.com

Northern Kentucky Property Owners Assoc.
Ft. Mitchell, KY.
859-261-9600
www.nkpoa.com

LOUISIANNA

New Orleans Real Estate Investors Assoc.
Metairie, LA.
504-833-8775
www.neworleansreia.com

Southwest Louisiana Real Estate Investors Club
Lake Charles, LA.
337-480-2522

MAINE

Maine Apartment Owners Assoc.
Hallowell, ME.
800-204-4311
www.maoma.org

Greater Portland Housing Assoc.
Portland, ME.
207-761-1764

Central Maine Apartment Owners Assoc.
Waterville, ME.
207-873-5471
www.cmaoa.com

Farmington Area Landlords and Managers Association
Bangor, ME.
207-469-3702

Bad Renters Network
207-453-4777
www.badrenters.net www.mrlandlord.com

Greater Bangor Owners and Managers Assoc.
Bangor, ME.
207-469-3702

RE Ventures
York Harbor, ME.
207-351-3366

MARYLAND

Baltimore Real Estate Investors Assoc.
Baltimore, MD.
410-583-7300
www.baltimorereia.com

Beltway Breakfast Club
Baltimore, MD.
410-644-0663

Capital Area REIA
Annapolis, MD.
571-261-2152
www.capitalareareia.com

Central Maryland REIA
Frederick, MD.
301-620-4036
301-218-4333
www.dcreia.com

Maryland Real Estate Exchange
Baltimore, MD.
443-253-3886
www.mdrealestateclub.com

Mid-Atlantic Real Estate Investor Assoc.
Baltimore, MD.
410-669-8375
www.mareria.com

Central Maryland Real Estate Investors Group
Bowie, MD.
202-783-0093

Real Estate Investors Club of Baltimore
Baltimore, MD.
410-661-9645
410-837-6667

Real Estate Invest Net
Mount Rainer
301-209-1899

MASSACHUSETTS

AREI North Mass.
Andover, MA.
877-932-5594 ext. 706

Bay State Wealth Builders
Dedham, MA.
508-580-5554 ext. 109
www.baystatewealthbuilders.com

Boston REIA
Waltham, MA.
866-378-3037
www.bostonareia.com

Cape Cod AREI
Bourne, MA.
877-773-5333
www.capecodarei.com

Financial Destination Inclusive Real Estate Assoc.
Andover, MA.
978-455-5493
www.fdireia.com

Mass. Real Estate Investors Assoc. & Apartment Owners Assoc.
Worcester, MA.
508-987-8806 ext. 705
www.massreia.com

Mass. REIA
Peabody, MA.
781-639-8616
www.massrealestate.com

Metro West Investors Group
Natick, MA.
508-533-1999

www.metrowestivestors.com

New England Real Estate Investors Assoc.
Chelmsford, MA.
603-887-0950

Northeast Real Estate investors Group
Stoughton, MA.
781-297-0202

MICHIGAN

Associated Landlords of Detroit
Oak Park, MI.
313-832-0523

Dollars (Wendy Patton)
248-628-6455

Genesse Landlords Assoc.
Flint, MI.
810-767-3080
www.geneseelandlordassoc.org

Kalamazoo Area Rental Housing Assoc.
Portage, MI.
616-383-4664

Lenawee Area Rental Housing Assoc.
Tipton, MI.
517-431-2041

My Real Estate Group
Westland, MI.

248-388-1680

National Real Estate Network
248-762-0800
Livonia, MI.
www.megaeveningevent.com

Real Estate Investor Assoc. of Macomb
Roseville, MI.
586-203-8333
www.reiaofmacomb.com

Real Estate Investor Assoc. of Oakland
Clawson. MI.
800-747-6742
www.reiaofoakland.com

Real Estate Investor Assoc. of Wayne County
Dearborn, MI.
313-386-7228

Real Estate Investors of Michigan
Grand Rapids, MI.
800-701-7762
www.reiofmi.com

Rental Property Owners Assoc.
Wyoming, MI.
800-701-7762
www.rpoaonline.org

Wealth Investor Network
Livonia, MI.
810-714-5335

www.cashflowmi.com

Windy City Round Table
Hazel Park, MI.
248-506-8364
www.wcrtdetroit.com

MINNESOTA

Indus Investor Club
Edina, MN.
952-921-5821

Minneapolis REIA
Hopkins, MN.
612-387-6258
www.mlsreia.com

Minnesota Real Estate Exchange
Bloomington, MN.
612-646-8465

Minnesota Real Estate Investors Assoc.
Minneapolis, MN.
612-490-3072

MISSISSIPI

Residential Investment Group
Jackson, MS.
601-212-8471
www.realestatesuccess.com

Wealth Builders of South Miss.
Biloxi, MS.
228-697-1803
www.wbsms.com

MISSOURI

Kansas City Investment Group
St. Louis, MO.
816-292-2822

Lake of the Ozarks Real Estate Investing
573-346-1309
Linn Creek, MO.

Mid America Assoc. of Real Estate Investors
Kansa City, MO.
816-523-4400
www.mareinet.com

Southwest Missouri REIA
Joplin, MO.
417-439-8961

St. Louis REIA
St. Louis, MO.
636-225-3370

The RGC Real Estate Network
St. Louis, MO.
314-733-0500

Wealth Improvement Network
St. Louis, MO.

314-477-3886
www.stlwin.com

MONTANA

Missoula Real Estate Investment Club
Missoula, MT.
406-240-7657
www.realestate.meetup.com

Big Sky Real Estate Investors Club
Billings, MT.
406-208-3488
www.thebric.org

NEBRASKA

Omaha REI
Omaha, NE.
402-680-1125
www.finance.groups.yahoo.com/group/omahareia/

NEVADA

INV Consulting
North Las Vegas, NV.
702-212-4370

Las Vegas Magic
Las Vegas, NV.
702-499-7103

Las Vegas REIA
Las Vegas, NV.

702-769-9872
www.lvreia.com

Millionaire Real Estate Investment Club
Las Vegas, NV.
701-769-9872
www.mreclv.com

Prosper REIA
Las Vegas, NV.
702-505-9953
www.prosperreia.com

Sierra Reno Exchangers
702-355-8425

NEW HAMPSHIRE

New Hampshire Property Owners Assoc.
603-881-3682

New Hampshire REIA
Manchester/Bedford, NH.
603-622-3766
www.nhreia.org

New Hampshire Real Estate Investors Group
Portsmouth, NH.
603-436-8226

NEW JERSEY

Garden State Apartments
Newark, NJ.

973-954-2787
www.gardenstateapartments.com

Garden State REIA
South Orange, NJ.
201-862-1443
www.gsreia.com

Metropolitan Investors Assoc.
Kenilworth, NJ.
201-791-4639
www.mreia.com

New Jersey Real Estate Investment Club
Paramus, NJ.
973-220-1179
www.njreclub.com

South Jersey Investors Inc.
Collingswood, NJ.
856-663-1133
www.southjerseyinvestors.com

Northern New Jersey Real Estate Investment Club
Passaic, NJ.
973-703-8503

NEW MEXICO

Capital Investment Group of New Mexico
Albuquerque, NM.
505-298-3900

IRIN Albuquerque Chapter
Albuquerque, NM.
505-250-3690
www.irin.net

Insiders Club
Santa Fe, NM.
505-472-5332

NEW YORK

Adirondack Creative Funding
Glens Falls, NY.
518-798-4374

Big Apple REIA
Bronx, NY.
718-654-2694
www.bigapplereia.com

Brooklyn REI Club
Brooklyn, NY.
917-345-3045

Central New York Investors Assoc.
New Hartford, NY.
315-264-9235
www.cnyia.com

Empire State Real Estate Investors Assoc.
Albany, NY.
518-449-3331

Greater Westchester REIA
New Rochelle, NY.
718-325-4112
www.gwreia.com

Long Island Investors Group
Melville, NY.
800-230-4280 ext. 200
www.lireia.com

Mid-Hudson Valley REI Club
Poughkeepsie, NY.
877-571-0918
www.husonvalleyreiclub.homestead.com

National Real Estate Symposium
New York, NY.
914-964-1177

New York City REIA
New York City, NY.
718-654-2694
www.nycreia.com

New York State REIA
Troy, NY.
518-786-8896
www.nyreia.com

Real Estate Investment Education Club
Levittown, NY.
516-298-4135
www.reiec.com

Real Estate Investors of Central New York
N. Syracuse, NY.
315-475-0701
www.reicny.org

Upstate New York Real Estate Investors
Rochester, NY.
585-697-4088
www.upstatenyreia.com

Western New York Real Estate Investors
Grand Island, NY.
716-773-2980

NORTH CAROLINA

Carolinas Real Estate Investors Assoc.
Asheville, NC.
828-252-0723

Central Carolina Real Estate Investors Assoc.
336-437-0851
Greensboro, NC.

Charlotte REIA
Charlotte, NC.
704-891-9619
www.charlottereia.com

Charlotte Early Risers Real Estate Investors
Charlotte, NC.
704-891-9619

Metrolina Real Estate Investors Assoc
Charlotte, NC.
704-536-8600
www.metrolinareia.com

Piedmont Triad REIA
Greensboro, NC.
336-399-7700

Triangle Real Estate Investors Assoc.
Morrisville, NC.
919-553-2244
www.treia.com

NORTH DAKOTA

(NO CLUBS)

OHIO

Akron REIA
Akron, OH.
330-644-2413
www.acreia.org

Ashtabula REIA
Ashtabula, OH.
440-964-8709
www.areia.com

Columbus Real Estate Buying and Investing
Columbus, OH.
614-367-0315

Fostoria Area Landlords
Fostoria, OH.
419-894-6547

Greater Dayton Real Estate Investors Assoc.
Beaver Creek, OH.
937-586-3726
www.gdreia.com

Real Estate Investors Assoc. Inc.
Cleveland, OH.
216-751-5000

REIA of Columbus
Columbus, OH.
614-475-5038
www.reiacolumbus.org

REIANO Plus (Cleveland)
Cleveland, OH.
216-651-6655
www.reiano.com

Southeastern Ohio REIA
Cambridge, OH.
740-432-2525
740-596-9551

Columbus Real Estate Exchangers
Columbus, OH.
614-890-1543

Muskingum Apartment Owners Assoc.
Zanesville, OH.

740-455-6442

REIA of Cincinnati
800-795-0083

Lake Erie Landlords Assoc.
Elyria, OH.
440-967-0045

OKLAHOMA

OKC REIA
Oklahoma City, OK.
405-650-1732
www.okcreia.com

Tulsa REIA
Tulsa, OK.
918-760-7303
www.tulsareia.com

VIP REIA
918-354-2645
www.realestateconnection.org

OK Properties
918-834-7355
Tulsa, OK.

OREGON

Northwest REIA
Portland, OR.
503-488-5969

www.northwestreia.com

Southern Oregon Rental Owners Assoc.
Medford, OR.
541-772-4180

Wealth Builders REIA
Portland, OR.
503-657-0245
www.wbreia.com

First Oregon NCE
Albany, OR.
503-931-1018

Creative Real Estate Strategies
Eugene, OR.
541-345-9902

Objective Real Estate
Eugene, OR.
541-688-7483

PENNSYLVANIA

ACRE of Pittsburg
Pittsburgh, PA.
888-422-7340

Central Region Residential Owners Assoc.
814-238-4967

Diversified Real Estate Investor Group
Plymouth Meeting, PA.

215-712-2525
www.digonline.org

Indiana County Rental Asoc.
Indiana, PA.
724-479-8642

Professional Organizers of Bucks County
215-493-9045

Western Pennsylvania REIA
Pittsburgh, PA.
412-382-5677
www.westernpareia.com

Wyoming Valley REIA
Wilkes Barre, PA.
610-398-9005

RHODE ISLAND

Rhode Island Real Estate Investors Group
Warwick, RI.
401-726-1300
www.northeastreia.com

South Carolina

Capitol City Real Estate Investors LLC.
Columbia, SC.
803-948-8033
www.screia.com

Foothills REIA
Spartanburg, SC.
864-205-9421
www.foothillsreia.com

South Carolina REIA
Myrtle Beach, SC.
843-997-4289
www.screia.com

Upstate Carolina REIA
Greenville, SC.
864-542-4202
www.upstatecreia.com

SOUTH DAKOTA

(NO CLUBS)

TENNESSEE

Knoxville Real Estate Investors Group
Knoxville, TN.
865-973-0366

Memphis Investors Group
Germantown, TN.
901-550-7181
www.memphisinvestorsgroup.com

Middle Tennessee Real Estate Investors
McMinnville, TN
931-6689-8080
www.realestate.meetup.com

North West Tennessee Real Estate Investors
Dyersburg, TN.
901-285-1333

Real Estate Investors of Nashville
Nashville, TN.
615-353-7056
www.reintn.net

Southeast Note Buyers
Knoxville, TN.
423-909-9831

Real Estate Investors of the Tri-States
Chattanooga, TN.
423-344-7807

TEXAS

Alamo Investors Assoc.
San Antonio, TX.
210-979-2626
www.alamoinvestors.com

Arlington Real Estate Assoc.
Arlington, TX.
817-371-8658
www.realestate.meetup.com/445/

Assoc. of Independent Real Estate Owners
Dallas, TX.
214-761-1996
www.aireo.org

Austin REI Club
Austin, TX.
512-301-9171

Bilingual REIA
Ft. Worth, TX.
817-47-0092

Brazos Valley Real Estate Investors Assoc
College Station
979-693-7883

Cedar Park Real Estate Club
Cedar Park, TX.
512-219-0996
www.cedarparkrealestateclub.com

Central Texas Investors Club
Waco, TX.
254-776-5888
www.centraltexasinvestorsclub.com

Clear Lake Investment Club LLC.
Houston, TX.
281-335-3938
www.clearlakeinvestmentclub.com

Clear Lake REIA
619-675-9809

Dallas Fort Worth Investor Network
Dallas, TX.
972-671-7346
www.dfwrein.com

Johnson County Area Real Estate Organizers
Burleson, TX.
817-975-0978
www.jcareio.com

Lifestyles Unlimited
Irving, TX.
972-827-0208
www.luinc.com

Money Roots Real Estate Investment Club
Killeen, TX.
254-449-7584
www.moneyroots.com

REI Club of Austin
AUSTIN, TX.
512-302-6771
www.yourreica.com

Real Estate Investment Club Training
Dallas, TX.
214-467-7355
www.reitc.com

Real Estate Investors Organization (REIO)
Fort Worth, TX.
817-73-0120
www.reio-fw.com

Realty Investment Club of Houston
Houston, TX.
713-947-7424
www.richclub.org

Real Estate Investment Organization
Amarillo, TX.
806-655-7976

REI of San Antonio
San Antonio, TX.
210-379-1636
www.reiosa.com

RGVREIC
Weslaco, TX.
956-631-4361

San Antonio REIA
San Antonio, TX.
210-662-0297
www.sareia.com

Texas Real Estate Investors Circle
Dallas, TX.
469-233-1722
www.texasrealestateinvestorscircle.com

UTAH

CWA
11075 S. State St. #29
Sandy UT. 84070
www.re90x.com

Fast Track Investments
Layton, UT.
801-390-7042
www.fasttrackinvestorsclub.com

Landlords Anonymous
Salt Lake City, UT.
801-250-6175

Wasatch Creative Real Estate Investors Assoc.
Salt Lake City, UT.
801-838-7989
www.wareia.com

Salt Lake REIA
Sandy, UT.
801-830-4830
www.slreia.com

Southern Utah REIA
St. George, UT.
435-632-9358
www.sureia.com

Tooele REIA
Salt Lake City, UT.
435-849-2140

Utah Creative Real Estate Assoc.
Salt Lake City, UT.
801-913-6195
www.ucrea.net

Weber County Real Estate Investment Club
Ogden UT.
801-399-9788

VERMONT

North Country Real Estate Investors
St. Johnsbury, VT.
802-748-2303

VIRGINIA

Capital Area REIA
Vienna, VA.
571-261-2152
www.capitalareareia.com

DC/Virginia Real Estate Investors Group
Chantilly, VA.
800-393-3138
www.dcvareig.com

Hampton Roads Real Estate Investment Group
Virginia Beach, VA.
757-270-4101

Northern Virginia Real Estate Investors Group
Alexandria, VA.
703-768-3325

Real Estate Community Networking Group
Alexandria, VA.
703-349-2934
www.realestatecng.com

Richmond REIA
Richmond, VA.
804-715-9415

www.rreia.org

Tidewater Real Estate Investors Group
Hampton, VA.
757-825-8759

Richmond Area Apartment Owners Assoc.
Richmond, VA.
804-358-4784

Richmond Creative Investors Assoc.
Richmond, VA.
804-269-7994

Virginia Foreclosure Club
804-966-1395

Roanoke Real Estate Investors
Roanoke, VA.
540-772-7605

Washington D.C.

National REIA-DC
www.dcreia.com

DC/Central Maryland Investors Group
202-783-0093 ext. 221
www.dcmreig.com

Real Estate Investors Club of Metro Washington
301-340-9399
www.reimw.com

Washington REIA Network
Bethesda, MD.
301-231-5437

WASHINGTON

Bellingham Real Estate Investor Network
Bellingham, WA.
800-691-3036
www.breinonline.org

Central Washington REIA
Yakima, WA.
509-480-0017
www.centralwashingtonreia.com

National Real Estate Investors Spokane
Spokane Valley, WA.
509-496-1026
www.finance.groups.yahoo.com/group/nrei-Spokane/

Northwest Real Investors Assoc.
Lynnwood, WA.
206-498-2350
www.nwria.com

Pierce Investors Club
Parkland, WA.

Real Estate Assoc. of Puget Sound
Seattle, WA.
425-458-4797
www.reapsweb.com

Real Estate Investors Assoc. of Washington
Bellevue, WA.
877-454-REIA
www.reiawa.com

The Real Estate Club
Tacoma, WA.
253-531-4000
www.realestateendeavor.com/the_real_estate_club.php

WEST VIRGINIA

West Virginia Landlords Assoc. of Kanawha Valley
Charleston, WV.
304-342-4342

West Virginia Landlords Assoc. of the Eastern Panhandle
Martinsburg, WV.
304-267-7210

WISCONSIN

Equity Builders
Eau Claire, WI.
715-833-5377

Fox Valley Real Estate Club
Appleton, WI.
920-428-9858
www.foxvalleyrealestategroup.com

Milwaukee Real Estate Investors Group
Milwaukee, WI.
608-807-4247
www.milwuakeering.com

WYOMING

Northern Utah Real Estate Investors
435-75-7995
Servicing Utah, Idaho, & Wyoming

CANADIAN GROUPS

Alberta Real Estate Investors Club
Calgary, AB.
403-688-8666 Ext. 66
www.albertareic.com

Canadian Real Estate Investment Group
Mississauga, ON.
905-272-9600
www.canreig.com

Canadian Real Estate Investors Group
Toronto, ON.
905-883-0135

Edmonton Revenue Property Investors Assoc.
Edmonton, AB.
780-433-1481

Le Club D'Investisseurs Immobiliers du Quebec
Montreal, QC.
514-608-8283

www.clubimmobilier.qc.ca

Midland Investment Group
Midland, ON.
705-526-4507

Monckton Real Estate Investors Organization
Monckton, NB.
506-387-4881

Nanaimo Real Estate Investors Club
250-588-3396
Nanaimo, BC.
www.nanaimorei.com

Okanogan Millionaire Real Estate Investors Club
250-309-9009
Vernon, BC.

Ottawa Real Estate Investors Organization
Ottawa, ON.
613-829-0888
www.oreio.org

Private Investment Club
Mississauga, ON.
888-302-6163
www.privateinvestmentclub.ca

Real Estate Investment Network-Edmonton
888-824-7346
Edmonton, AB.
www.albertsrein.com

Real Estate Investment Network-Calgary
403-208-2722
Calgary, AB.

Real Estate Investment Network-Ontario
Toronto, ON.
888-824-7346
www.ontariorein.com

Real Estate Investment Club of Ontario
London, ON.
519-619-0809

Refocus Real Estate Investing-Edmonton
Edmonton, AB.
780-490-7320

Regina REIA
Regina, Sask.
306-539-5306

Real Estate Investors League
Waterloo, ON.
519-699-4340

Real Estate Investment Networking Group
Oakville, ON.
905-469-7448
www.helpingeachother.ca

Real Estate Action Group
604-683-3870
Vancouver, BC.

Toronto Real Estate Investment Netwrok
Toronto, ON.
416-243-9900

Victoria Real Estate Investment Club
Toronto, ON.
416-464-2652
www.preigcanada.com

Women Investing In Real Estate
Calgary, AB.
403-71-7355

Wealth Investment Networking Group
Calgary, AB.
403-278-9061

DISCLAIMER

Although the authors and publisher have made every effort to ensure that the information in this book was correct at press time, the authors and publisher do not assume and hereby disclaim any liability to any party for any loss, damage, or disruption caused by errors or omissions, whether such errors or omissions result from negligence, accident, or any other cause.

(Case study with Tasha)

Appendix I: Checklists & Worksheets

On The TV shows you never see the paperwork that is being used, and what steps exactly are taken in preparation for the purchase or sell of a property. Paperwork is a BIG part of the business, and checklists are critical. Some now use their smart phone or tablet to eliminate lose papers stacking up, but either way is sufficient.

We have attached the most common worksheets and checklists that are used in today's real estate market. Keep in mind you are looking to gather the appropriate information for the property, which will give you enough information to calculate the offer and repair costs.

What you intend to do with the property is very important. Remember this sequence for your business: locate, evaluate, negotiate, contracts, financing, and exit strategy. Stay in this path of progression and you will always be on track.

Attic Checklist

1.Insulation	Type
	Amount
	Location
	Condition (Damaged, needs to be replaced)
	Comments:
2. Leaks	Around the chimney (yes/no)
	Vent pipe leaks (yes/no)
	Daylight visible from attic (yes/no)
	Location
	Comments:
3. Ventilation	Kind *(gable, roof, ridge, soffit)*
	Needs repairs (yes/no)
	Sufficient ventilation (yes/no)
	Sips of condensation (yes/no)
	Comments:
4. Improper Venting Into Attic	Location *(bathroom vents, kitchen vents)*
	Comments:
5. Framing	Condition (*structurally sound, insect activity, decaying)*
	Comments:

Basement Checklist

1.Water Penetration	Location
	Efflorescence (yes/no)
	Sump pump working (yes/no)
	Comments:
2. Cellar Floor:	Condition *(holes, evidence of water, cracks, needs repairs)*
	Comments:
3. Foundation Walls:	Accessible, inaccessible
	Condition *(poor, fair, good)*
	Comments:
4. Main Girder:	Condition *(resting on foundation, needs repairs)*
	Evidence of deterioration, decay or insect activity (yes/no) Extent:
	Comments:
5. Insect Activity:	Type.
	Extent of damage
	Location
	Comments:
6. Floor Joists:	Condition *(damaged, decaying, rotting, sagging)*
	Comments:
7. Posts:	Type
	Condition *(fair, good, needs repairs)*
	Comments:
8. Insulation:	Type
	Condition
	Location
	Amount of insulation
	Vapor barrier (yes/no)
	Comments:
9. Crawl Spaces: (yes/no)	Location
	Condition
	Comments:

Bathroom Checklist

Fixtures:	Condition *(poor, fair, good)*
	Leaks (yes/no)
	Damaged or chipped fixtures (yes/no)
	Faucets dripping (yes/no)
	Comments:
Ventilation:	Type *(mechanical vents, windows)*
	Comments:
Ceilings:	In need of repairs (yes/no)
	Comments:
Ground Fault Interrupter:	Yes/no
	Is it working (yes/no)
	Comments:
Water Pressure:	Adequate, needs repairs
	Comments:
Tile:	Condition *(missing, chipped, broken, falling off of walls)*
	Comments:
Heat:	Yes/no
	Comments:
Floors:	Condition (*tile pulling up, needs replacement, deteriorating or decaying)*
	Comments:
Walls:	Condition *(damaged walls from water, needs repairs, loose plaster)*
	Comments:
Drainage:	Normal, sluggish
	Comments:

Contractor Policy and Procedure Sample

There are no exceptions to the following policies and procedures:

- All contracts must be in writing and as detailed as possible.
- No checks will be issued without written contracts and invoices.
- Regarding draws, a maximum of 1/3 (one-third) of the total bid will be given up front to cover materials. The balance will not be paid until all work is complete. Absolutely complete. If one doorknob is loose, or one sink has a small leak, the balance will not be paid.
- The balance will not be paid until all of the contractors trash is removed.
- Service calls will not be paid until they are completed and verified by the tenant that they are complete.
- Contractor will give a date for the completion of a job. If the job is not complete, then the landlord loses money by not being able to rent out the property. Therefore, a $50.00 per day penalty will be deducted from the contractor's final draw for each day, including weekends, that the job is not done.
- On houses for Section 8, 20% of the total will be held back until the unit passes the Section 8 inspection.
- A $25.00 bonus will be paid for units that pass the Section 8 inspection the first time.
- Contractor will guarantee work for six months.
- Contractor must show proof of Workman's Compensation insurance. If not, the premiums will be deducted from the cost of the job and paid by the owner or property manager.
- All contractors must sign and agree to this contractor's agreement and attached agreement regarding liability and contractor's status as a contractor and not an employee.

OWNER MANAGER CONTRACTOR

_______________________ _______________________

Disclosure Statement (Realtor)

DISCLOSURE

I, ______________ acknowledge that _________________ is a licensed real estate agent with COMPANY NAME and is buying/selling this property for investment purposes. I further acknowledge that ________________ may rent out or resell this property at a later date for a profit.

I agree to hold _________________ and COMPANY NAME harmless for any claims that I may have regarding this contract. Also, I acknowledge that neither ____________ or COMPANY NAME represents me or my interests.

DATE___________________________

BUYER__________________________

SELLER_________________________

Examine Exterior Checklist

Foundation:	Type
	Condition *(missing mortar in joints, open holes, cracks, other damage)*
	Comments:
Roof:	Type
	Shingles (missing pieces, cracking, damage)
	Framing (bowed sheathing, sagging ridge)
	Comments:
Windows:	Type
	Condition (*caulking needed, broken glass, missing putty, missing latches)*
	Comments:
Chimney:	Condition *(missing mortar, damaged bricks, crumbling or cracking brickwork)*
	Flashing *(cemented over, open gaps or holes, needs overall repair)*
	Comments:
Trim:	Condition *(decaying wood, missing sections, peeling or chipped paint)*
	Comments:
Gutters:	Type
	Condition *(leaking, decaying, damaged, cracked)*
	Comments:

Exterior Checklist (continued)

Siding:	Type
	Condition *(decaying, cracked, dented, damaged)*
	Repairs required *(peeling paint, rusting, replace or repair missing sections)*
	Comments:
Downspouts:	Type
	Condition *(open seams, missing sections, rusting)*
	Discharging to foundation (yes/no)
	Comments:
Roof Vents:	Flashing *(defective, needs repairs, leaking)*
	Condition *(broken, damaged, missing)*
	Comments:
Entrances:	Condition of doors *(fair, good, needs repairs)*
	Condition of steps *(decaying, deteriorating brickwork, unsafe for use)*
	Rails (yes/no)
	Comments:
Foundation Windows:	Type
	Condition *(decaying, rusting, broken)*
	Comments:
Porches:	Location
	Condition *(decaying or damaged wood, sips of wood-boring insects, need for repairs)*
	Comments:
Skylights:	Damage *(missing putty, cracked glass, decaying or damaged frame)*
	Comments:

Exterior Checklist (continued)

Garage:	Attached/Detached
	Condition (*needs repairs, winterizing)*
	Comments:
Driveway:	Condition (*cracking, decaying, heaving)* Needs repairs *(minor, major)*
	Comments:
Low Wood Members:	Location.
	Condition *(decaying, insect activity, needs replacement)*
	Comments:
Grade:	Does surface water flows toward house/building(location ________________)
	Drywalls (yes/no)
	Possibility of flooding (yes/no)
	Comments:
Energy Losses:	Location(s)
	Type(s) *(open gaps in siding, loose or missing trim, trim needs caulking, weather-stripping needed around windows and doors)*
	Comments:
Landscaping:	Overgrown shrubs (yes/no)
	Ivy on house (yes/no)
	Overhanging tree branches (yes/no)
	Location
	Comments:
Fences:	Type.
	Condition *(rusting, decaying)*
	Comments:
Retaining Wall:	Types
	Weep holes (yes/no)

Exterior Checklist (continued)

	Condition *(decaying, needs repair)*
	Comments:
Paths:	Condition *(settled, unsafe to use, cracked, damaged)*
	Comments:
Structural Pests:	Sips of (*carpenter ants, termites, cockroaches, powder-post beetles)*
	Location of damage
	Comments:

Fireplace Checklist

1. Safety Hazards:	Location
	Types
	Comments:
2. Condition of Flue Pipe:	Poor, fair, good, needs replacement
	Comments:
3. Last Cleaning and Servicing Date:	Comments:
4. Needs Cleaning:	Yes/No
	Comments:
5. Permit for Stove:	Yes/No
	Comments
6. Proximity to Combustible Materials:	Location
	Comments:

Kitchen Checklist

Stove:	Type of fuel *(electricity, gas, oil)*
	Unit working (yes/no)
	Comments:
Sink:	Condition *(poor, fair, good)*
	Piping *(damaged, leaks, needs replacement)*
	Comments:
Ceilings:	Condition
	Comments:
Appliances:	Types
	Ages
	Condition
	Working (yes/no)
	Comments:
Walls:	Need repairs (yes/no)
	Comments:
Floors:	Needs replacement (yes/no)
	Comments:
Ventilation and Light:	Adequate, inadequate
	Comments:
Heat:	Yes/No
	Comments:
Cabinets and Counter Space:	Adequate, inadequate
	Comments:
Electrical Outlets:	Sufficient, need more outlets
	Comments:

Property Acquisition Worksheet

ADDRESS: ____________________

____

Estimated Sales Price After Fix-Up $ ____________

Down Payment	
Closing Costs	
Commission	
Appraisal	
Termite	
Miscellaneous	
Total Expense to Buy	

Rehab Budget	
Cost Overruns (+/-10%)	
Total Rehab Costs	

Payments for _____ Months	
Property Tax	
Insurance	
Total Holding Costs (+your time & cost of your capital)	

Sale Closing Costs	
Commission	
Advertising, telemarketing	
Total Sales Costs	

$ Mortgage Pay-offs	
Total Sales Price-	
Expense to Buy-	
Total Rehab Costs-	
Total Holding Costs-	
Total Sales Costs-	

Your Profit=

Rehab Worksheet

1. CASH OUT OF POCKET	
Down Payment	
Closing Costs	
Appraisal	
Termite letter	
Survey	
Title Ins.	
Misc.	
TOTAL:	
2. COST OF REHAB:	
Flooring	
Painting	
Roofing	
Windows/Screens	
Kitchen (faucets, cabinets, etc.)	
Bathroom (vanity, sink, tub, etc.)	
Bedrooms	
Decorations (ceiling fans, brass, etc.)	
Doors	
Foundation	
Fireplace	
Plumbing	
Insulation	
Subtotal: Total multiplied by a 15% repair cost overrun:	
TOTAL:	
3. ESTIMATED HOLDING COSTS:	
# Months x Mtge.______	
+ Ins.______	
+ Taxes______	
+ Util.______	
TOTAL:	
4. ESTIMATED SELLING COSTS (following rehab):	
Closing Costs	
Attorneys fees	
Document/Transfer taxes	

Rehab Worksheet (continued)

Commissions	
TOTAL:	
5. TOTAL EST. ACQUISITION, REHAB & SELLING COSTS (Add totals from 1,2,3):	
5a. Plus (+) Mortgage Balance Payoff:	
6. TOTAL COST OF PROPERTY (Add lines 5 and 5a):	
7. TOTAL PROJECTED SELLING PRICE (following rehab):	
8. TOTAL PROFIT (Subtract Line 6 from Line 7)	

PROPERTY INFORMATION WORKSHEET

Property Address Referred by:
City State Zip

Map/Parcel Legal Trust Deed Book Page Deed Book/Page
Current Owner: Phone Spouse
Date Purchased Purchase Price

Mortgage Amount Interest Rate %
Years Amortized P&I Last Payment Made
Approximate Balance # of Elapsed Payments

Amount Needed to Re-instate Pay-Off Amount
Mortgage Co. Contact Phone
Foreclosure Date Trustee Phone

2nd Mortgage Held By Contact Phone
Amount Int. Rate Date Originated Book Page
Approximate Balance Account#
Trustee Phone

3rd Mortgage Held By Contact Phone
Amount Int. Rate Date Originated Book Page
Approximate Balance Account
Trustee Phone

Lien: Amount $ Date Book/Page
Metro Liens: Amount $ Date Book/Page
IRS Liens:Amount $ Date Book/Page
Contact Phone
State Tax Liens: Amount $ Date Book/Page
Contact Phone

Bankruptcy: Chapter Date Filed Case#
SS# Attorney Phone
Date Discharged/Dismissed Relief From Automatic Stay Granted
Neighbor Phone Neighbor Phone
Other Family Member(s) Phone

NOTES:

2

Conclusion

These are just a small amount of the worksheets and checklists you can use in your real estate business. Many forms and documents are used daily and throughout your business regardless of your experience level. Staying up to date on new additions to your local laws and regulations is very important, since that may or may not alter your worksheets and checklists.

As you have seen throughout this book, jamming all the information to complete one property, or run a real estate investing business, can't be placed into a one episode of a reality show. The content of this business can't be placed in a 10 episode season. To film one season of a series on cable, they take 40 hours of film, cut, splice, paste, and alter to get 10 segments of 20 minutes in length. There is a foundation of knowledge required in this business, which involves, market data, laws, regulations, an understanding of financial participation, and so much more.

Now you can see that the glitz and glamour of the business is all hype from producers and not the real facts of how to start a real estate business, and sustain the business long term. We believe in the facts and being REAL. Real Estate is REAL. You need time, motivation, and energy to be successful.

This book was written to help you, regardless of your experience level, to Learn from the mistakes of others and build a stronger foundation of knowledge. The market has changed now, and you must have knowledge of this business, that is often overlooked, when you hear about buying and selling real estate.

Take advantage of the other resources we have available for you to create wealth in real estate

With real estate, as with most activities in life, reading just a few books will not give you all you need, to be successful. Although the real estate has had ups and downs, in the last few years, it still remains historically more stable and dependable than many of the other financial opportunities available today. This is the one business that you still don't need money or credit to be successful.

Success leaves clues! We have numerous resources to help both the beginner and seasoned investor. Follow this simple quote:

"The book you don't read can't help you."

Sincerely,

Brad & Chad

For more information on our team, books, materials, partner opportunities, and seminars in your area, please register online at our website www.RE90x.com, and receive additional evaluation sheets, flow charts, and so much more.

Real People . Real Deals . Real Success

Find us on: facebook.

What are people saying about us?

"These guys are the most genuine and trustworthy guys I have been around in a long time. Very knowledgeable and savvy in all areas of Real Estate, and are an huge asset to anyone." *–Robert Hightower CAR, NAR*

"They have added a rocket booster to our business, and the training has been amazing." *–Jed Gibson, NAMB*

"My wife and I realized these guys truly care about us accomplishing our goals, and aren't in this just for themselves. It's honestly like having your best friends right next to you going over everything with you and walking you through the business." *-Ken and Teri*